Published in Great Britain by The Reader's Digest Association Limited
Berkeley Square House
Berkeley Square
London W1X 6AB

Volume copyright © 1995 by Breslich & Foss
Illustrations copyright © 1995 by Lyndsay Milne

Conceived and produced by Breslich & Foss
20 Wells Mews
London W1P 3FJ

Project editors: Janet Ravenscroft and Catriona Woodburn
Art director: Nigel Osborne
Designers: Sally Stockwell and Paul Cooper
Photography by Nigel Bradley at Visuel 7 and George Zawadzki at Studio Z

ISBN 0 276 42184 1

A CIP catalogue record for this book is available from the British Library.

Printed in Spain
Typeset by Type Technique, London W1
Colour reproduction by Regent

LYNDSAY MILNE

fun FACTORY

GAMES AND TOYS FROM HOUSEHOLD RUBBISH

Reader's Digest

Published by The Reader's Digest Association Limited

LONDON • NEW YORK • SYDNEY • CAPE TOWN • MONTREAL

Contents

Introduction

Fun Factory is all about making exciting and original toys and games from ordinary household items like cardboard boxes, old newspapers, plastic bottles and aluminium foil. Recycling unwanted bits and pieces like these helps save your pocket money as well as natural resources. Instead of having to save up for weeks to buy one thing from a toyshop, you can make something unique in a few hours. Most of these projects can be completed in one afternoon – those that take longer, such as the castle and the island town, are clearly indicated.

The most important thing you'll need is cardboard. So that you don't end up with lots of boxes cluttering up the house, undo the seams and store them flat. (Very large boxes often have stapled edges. Be careful when taking out the staples so that you don't get scratched.) Cardboard is the bulkiest thing that you're going to need. Keep smaller items such as toilet-roll tubes, yoghurt cartons, beads and pieces of fabric in a big box so that you don't lose them. This way, you won't have to spend hours rummaging around the house when you want to get on with making a puppet theatre or whatever it is.

Throughout *Fun Factory* you will find **Green Facts**. These are snippets of information about the way we are damaging the environment by wasting natural resources and creating pollution. As everybody knows, the environment – the air we breathe, the water we drink – is very important. If we ruin it, we won't get another one. The good news is that there are ways in which we can limit the harm being done to the Earth, and re-using as many products as possible is one of them. When something is finished or empty, such as a tub of margarine or a bottle of detergent, don't think of it as rubbish to be thrown away, but as building material that you can use for one of your projects. Here's a list of the sort of things you should be looking out for and intercepting on their way to the dustbin.

6

Things to Collect

Stock cube boxes
Toothpaste tube boxes
Matchboxes
Eggboxes
Toilet-roll tubes
Kitchen-roll tubes

Paper
Plain white paper
Coloured paper
Large brown envelopes
White envelopes
Tissue paper
Sweet wrappers
Paper bags
Paper plates
Drinking straws
Baking cases
Greaseproof paper
Newspapers
Magazines
Wallpaper

Plastic
Detergent bottles
Shampoo bottles
Cosmetics bottles

Mineral water bottles
Cordial bottles
5-litre (8½ pint) container, with handle
Plastic screw-on bottle tops
Yoghurt cartons
Margarine tubs
Large plastic bags
Small sandwich bags
Cellophane
Drinking straws
Toothpaste
   tube caps
Eggboxes

Cardboard
Thin and thick cardboard
Corrugated cardboard

Cereal boxes
Washing powder boxes
Shoe boxes

Glass
Jam jars
Bottles

Metal
Aluminium foil
Paint cans
Tin cans

Bottle tops
Foil trays from take-away meals
Jar lids
Foil sweet wrappers
Electrical wire
Coat hangers

Textiles
Old clothes
Sheets
Socks
Tights and stockings
Cotton thread
Ribbons
String
Elastic
Plain and patterned fabric
Furry fabric
Beads
Buttons
Sequins

Wood
Wooden spoons
Ice-lolly sticks
Used and unused matches
Cocktail sticks
Cane

Other bits and pieces
Cotton wool
Eggshells
Walnut shells
Stud paper-fasteners

Paper clips
Hose piping
Elastic bands
Pipe cleaners
Scouring pads
Corks
Sponge
Plasticine
Marbles

Materials

Pens and pencils
Black pencil
Coloured pencils
Coloured crayons
Ball-point pens
Felt-tipped pens
Black marker pen

Paint
All of the projects use water-based poster paints and powder paints, which are widely available from children's activity and craft stores.

Glue
Water-based hobby glue, also known as Marvin medium, school glue or water-based wood glue, can be used for gluing large surfaces and is good on cardboard and paper. To stick together fabric, glues like UHU or Bostik are best because they are easier to handle.

Tape
Masking tape is stronger and easier to paint over than sellotape.

You can make your own double-sided tape by cutting a strip of sellotape and winding it around your fingers, sticky side out, until the two ends meet. Remove it from you fingers and use it to join cardboard.

Basic Tool Kit

These are the things you will need for most projects. If you need anything else you will see it like this: **Extra item:** pump-action hairspray.

Pencil
Crayons
Felt-tipped pens
Marker pens
Water-based poster paints
   and powder paints
Paintbrushes
Masking tape

Glue
Scissors
Ruler

Handy Hints

CURLING PAPER AND PLASTIC

Curl strips of paper or thin plastic by holding the strip in one hand and running a closed pair of scissors or a spoon handle down and away from you with the other hand.

TIP

You can use closed scissor points to make a hole in cardboard. It is best to use scissors with round ends and never put your hand under the hole you are making! If you only have pointed scissors, ask a grown-up for help.

TIP

Use a hole punch instead of scissors for making holes for string ties in thin cardboard or paper.

PAINTING ON CARDBOARD BOXES

Some cardboard boxes – cereal boxes for example – have a lot of heavy printing on them that is difficult to paint over. The solution is to undo the box, turn it inside out and stick it back together with double-sided tape so that you have a plain surface to paint on.

MAKING AN EYE TEMPLATE

To make a personalised eye template hold a piece of paper in front of your face. Put your finger where one eye is and very carefully make a mark there with a pencil. Without moving the paper, do the same with the other eye. Remove the paper. Cut out eyeholes just big enough for you to see through and use this as a template for all masks.

TIP

When a project calls for plain white paper try not to use fresh paper. Ask grown-ups to give you any documents they have finished with and use the backs of letters. Cut shapes out of clean parts of discarded pieces of paper and envelopes or paint over writing.

DRAWING A PERFECT CIRCLE

The simplest way to draw a perfect circle is to trace around a mug or a plate. Another way is to make a compass. Cut a piece of string as wide as you would like your circle to be. Tie it at the middle around a pencil. Stick the string to a piece of paper with a drawing pin and move the pencil round so that you draw a circle.

PAINTING ON PLASTIC

It is difficult to paint on plastic with water-based poster paints – the paint just slides off! To help make the paint stick, prepare the plastic by rubbing it with fine sandpaper then spraying it with a thin layer of hairspray. Use pump-action hairspray – this doesn't contain the chlorofluorocarbons (CFCs) that damage the ozone layer. Let the hairspray dry before applying paint. If you don't have any hairspray, sandpaper the plastic a little harder to make the surface nice and rough.

MAKING NOSES

Here are two ways to make a simple nose for masks:

1 Draw an open-ended triangle on a face. Cut around the lines leaving the nose shape attached at the top. Cut a strip of thin card and bend one end up and attach it inside the nose. Bend the other end down and tape it inside the mask.

TIP
Where a project calls for used matches, ask a grown-up to burn them for you.

2 Cut a triangle out of card and fold it in half. Cut another strip of card, bend the ends over, and stick them inside the nose. Tape the nose to your mask.

TIP
To make things shiny and a little more hard-wearing mix up some water-based glue. Mix up half water and half glue and brush it on to dry paint surfaces. (If you have used felt-tipped pens to colour the item, test the piece first as some felt-tips run.) It is like painting with milk! Don't worry about white patches as they will dry clear. Small objects can be glazed with clear nail varnish.

MAKING A HEADBAND

Here's how to make a headband out of cardboard, elastic or string:

Measure your head with a tape-measure or piece of string to see how big it is. Cut a strip of thick card, string or elastic to this length. Tape or tie it securely so that the headdress or mask you attach it to won't slip off your head.

TIP

It is often a good idea to cut things out with tabs on them. You can then push the tab through slots in the thing you are making, bend them over and tape them down on the inside.

TIP

Always rinse paintbrushes thoroughly with cold water before putting them away so that they will be ready for use next time you need them.

TIP

Keep an old shirt to wear over your clothes when you are painting. If you do get paint on yourself, let it dry because then it will crack and is easy to peel off. Wash off any remaining paint with warm soapy water.

MAKING PAPIER MACHE

To make papier mâché, rip up some sheets of newspaper. Tear them into small pieces if you have to cover a small area and big pieces for a large area. Mix some flour and water together until it is as thick as a very thick milk shake. (You can also use wallpaper paste, but this takes longer to dry.) Drench the newspaper pieces in the flour-and-water paste then apply them. Build up two or three layers then leave the papier mâché to dry overnight.

Ark and Animals

In the story of the flood, the animals went into Noah's ark in pairs, to escape drowning and extinction. Today, animals in danger of extinction are sometimes taken out of the wild and put into captivity where they are encouraged to breed.

RECYCLE:

For the Ark
Shoe-box
Thin cardboard
Corrugated cardboard
Plasticine (or coins and a paper bag)
Small cardboard box

Extra item:
a small plate

For the Sheep
Used matches
Bottle cork
Cap off a toothpaste tube
Plain white or coloured paper

For the Tortoise
Halved walnut shells
Plain white and green paper

For the Hippopotamus
Thin cardboard

ARK

1 To make the base of the ark, take a shoebox and remove the lid. On one of the long sides of the box, use scissors to cut two slits 5 cm (2 in) apart down to the base.

2 For the bow and stern, cut out two identical pieces of card that are about 5 cm (2 in) longer, and 2.5 cm (1 in) higher than the long side of the box. Lay your box along the bottom of each piece. Mark the height of the top corners "X".

3 On each piece, rule a straight line from one edge of the card to the other, through the points you have marked "X". Next, fold both pieces of card exactly in half. Unfold, and mark the middle point "M". Draw a curve from "M" to each side. The curve should end where you have marked the "X" rule.

4 Cut along the curves you have drawn. At each edge, cut out a small rectangle. Now you should have two pieces of card the same shape as in the picture above.

5 Fold the two pieces of card down the middle again, to form points. With tape, stick the sides of the card to the shorter ends of the shoe-box to make the bow and stern.

6 To make decks for the bow and stern, place first the bow end, and then the stern end, on pieces of card and draw around them. Cut out triangles and tape them to the bottom of the ark.

7 So that the ark can rock, cut out two semi-circles of corrugated card. Do this by drawing around a small plate. Cut out the circle, and then cut it in half. Fix these with masking tape to the bottom of the ark, at either end of the shoe-box base. Reinforce them if necessary with extra card.

8 Weight the boat with plasticine or coins in a paper bag. Tape the bag or place the plasticine in the middle of the shoe-box. Paint the ark.

Keep the animals inside the shoe-box part of the ark when they are not being used.

9 To make the cabin, find a small box that fits well on the middle of the shoe-box lid. Cut out three sides of a door, that will open and shut. Cut out a rectangle for a window.

10 Cut out two identical rectangles of corrugated card to make the cabin roof. The length of these should be the same as the longer sides of the cabin box, and the height should be about three-quarters of the width of your box. Tape these together on the underside into a "V".

11 Tape the roof to the top of your box. Paint and decorate the cabin. You could add a chimney, curtains, flowers, or whatever you like. When the paint is dry, glue the cabin to the lid of the shoe-box.

SHEEP

1 Cut four used matches to about three-quarters of their original length. The burnt ends form the sheep's hooves. Push two match pieces in at each end of a cork to make the legs. (If the cut ends are slightly pointed, they will be easier to push in.) For a tail, cut a short piece off a fifth used match, and push this in.

2 Glue the cap to the head end of the animal. Paint the body and head. While this is drying, cut out small circles of paper for eyes and ears. Colour these and glue them to the head.

Paint the body and head white to make sheep, or turn them into cows by painting them brown all over or brown with white patches.

Green Fact: Paper and paper products are "biodegradable" and can be broken down by bacteria – unlike plastic, say, which is not "biodegradable", does not break down well and pollutes the environment.

TORTOISE

1 For the head and legs of the tortoise, cut out five paddle shapes from pieces of green paper. Cut out a small, pointed tail. With a black pen, draw marks for feet on the legs, and a smiling mouth. Cut out tiny circles for eyes and colour these.

2 Stick the legs onto the underside of the half walnut shell. Position all the legs so that they point backwards. Stick on the tail and eyes.

Walnut shells make excellent tortoises. If you have pistachio shells, you could make ants!

HIPPOPOTAMUS

1 Fold a piece of thin card in half. On one side, imagining the fold of the card to be the animal's back, draw the side view of your hippo – its short neck, legs, stomach and rear.

2 Keeping the card folded, cut around the shape you have drawn – through both thicknesses of card. If you prefer, trace the outline of the body shown below on to card, and cut that out.

3 Draw a head, like the one above (or trace the one shown below). Paint both body and head. When dry, draw on eyes, ears, mouth, nostrils and feet. You might like to paint on pink lips and toenails. Tape the head to the body.

If you prefer, you can trace this template for the hippopotamus. You can also adapt this pattern to make all sorts of other animals: you simply have to mark a crease down the centre of your card and draw a mirror image on each side.

Jungle

This jungle is not hard to make, and it looks brilliant. It will take about an afternoon and, as there is no need to let it dry overnight, it can be played with almost immediately. With the door-tie and the handle it can be carried around with all the animals, trees and leaves stored inside. As so many different kinds of animals, birds and insects live in the jungle, you can fill your model with almost anything you like. Decorate it with brightly coloured butterflies and tropical flowers.

RECYCLE:
For the Jungle
Medium-sized cardboard box
Cardboard
String
For the Leaves and Animals
Cardboard
For the Trees
Screw-tops from plastic bottles

Extra items: newspaper, potato

1 Choose one of the two largest sides of the box to be the front. Carefully cut this side off – keeping it in one piece. Cut this piece in half to make two doors.

2 Cut out two or three spiky-edged holes in the middle of each door. On three sides of each, cut spiky edges to look like leaves. Tape the straight edges to either side of the front of the box.

3 Cut out a thin piece of card the same size as the front opening of the box. This will make the jungle floor. Leaving one of the longest sides straight, cut the three other sides so that they are wavy. Tape the straight edge to the front edge of the box.

21

4 To make the divisions for the box, first cut two strips of card, about 5 cm (2 in) wide and the same length as the width across the box (marked "y" in the top picture). Next, cut three strips, also 5 cm (2 in) wide, but the same length as the height of the box (marked "x" in the top picture).

5 Measure the long strips. Divide by four. Mark off this new measurement. You should have three marks. For the shorter strips, measure and divide by three. You should end up with just two marks. Everywhere you have made a mark, cut a slot three-quarters of the way through the width of the card.

6 Line up your two long strips, with the slots facing upwards. Fit the shorter strips, with their slots facing downwards, into them. After painting (see step 7), put the "grid" you have made into the back of the box.

7 Lay out some newspaper. Paint the whole box green. If you are making leaves for the jungle (see below), paint these now. Take out the grid from the back of the box and paint it. On the jungle floor you could paint a pool of water for the animals to drink from.

8 Cut a potato in half. Draw a leaf sprig on to one half. Cut away the surrounding potato so that your design is raised. Dip this in dark-green paint and print leaves all over the box. Leave to dry.

9 Use scissor points to punch holes in the doors and top. To make a tie that will keep the front closed, thread a short piece of string through each of the door holes, knotting each piece on the inside. Knot thicker string on the insides of the holes in the top to make a carrying handle.

LEAVES

1 Cut out leaf shapes in card. Be sure they have a stem so that you can slot them into your box. You could make a few without stems, to stick at the back of the box where the partitions of the grid cross. Paint the leaves.

2 With closed scissors, carefully make slots in the sides and top of the box. These need to be wide enough for the leaf stems to fit in.

TREES

ANIMALS

1 Using the newspaper on which you painted your box, cut out a piece about 13 x 25.5 cm (5 x 10 in). With the painted side showing, roll it up – not too tightly – and secure it with a piece of tape.

2 Place one scissor point right down the centre of the tube, to be sure of cutting through all the layers of paper. Make four cuts, each to about a third of the way down. Now, pulling from the middle, gently twist out the paper. Bend down the branches. Glue the tree into a plastic bottle-top so that it will stand up.

1 Draw and colour various animals on thin card. You can copy this gorilla, or some of the animals on the previous pages – or make up your own. Cut them out.

2 Cut a strip of card to use as a support. Bend over one end and tape it to the back to complete your animal.

Masks and Costumes

Masks are great fun to make and look wonderful. As well as the large masks shown here, you can make smaller accessories: spectacles, funny noses, beards and headdresses. See which ideas appeal to you on the following pages and make up your own designs. Apart from boxes and cardboard, pots and cartons of all sizes are good to recycle for smaller masks.

24

RECYCLE:
Cardboard boxes
Corrugated cardboard
Thick and thin cardboard
Coloured paper (or plain paper and paints)
Large plastic bottles
Paper plate
Large brown envelope
Elastic
String

Aluminium foil, buttons, bottle tops
Coat hangers
Drinking straw

Extra items:
sandpaper, pump-action hairspray

HORSE MASK

Large cereal box
Strong card min. 60 x 4 cm (24 x 1½ in)

This horse mask is made from one large cereal box and a little extra cardboard for the ears and teeth. To make one like this, you will need white, pink, brown and black paint. You could also adapt the shape to make a dragon with fiery nostrils or a unicorn.

1 Keeping the open end of the box at the top, draw the shape for your horse's head down one long side. From the top, start to cut around the curved side of the shape you have drawn. When you get to the bit that forms the nostrils, cut off and discard the bulk of the box.

2 Continue to cut around the nostrils, but keep the whole of the bottom end of the box attached to the long straight side. This should not be cut. Repeat on the other side of the box. Wrap the end of the box around the horse's nose and mouth in a smooth curve. Tape securely.

3 Cut a long strip of card about 7.5 cm (3 in) thick, that can be bent into a horse-shoe shape and fitted in to give your horse teeth. Paint it white with black stripes. Glue it in place. Cut out cardboard ears and eyes. Paint the whole of the head.

4 Cut a long strip, about 4 cm (1½ in) wide, from strong cardboard. Put it around your head and tape it so that it fits snugly. Paint this. Use more tape to attach the horse's head to the band.

Green Fact: There are many advantages to recycling: less energy is used in the creation of new products; there is less pollution from factories and the dumping of waste; and money is saved when fewer new raw materials are imported.

BIRD MASK

Thin cardboard approx. 30 x 35 cm
  (12 x 14 in), and further pieces for
  the features
Corrugated or other strong card approx.
  60 x 4 cm (24 x 1½ in)
Coloured paper or plain white paper
  and paint

Make sure that the eyeholes are large enough to let you see out clearly. Cut a fat worm-shape out of cardboard. Paint it stripey and, when dry, tuck it into the front of the beak. Or tape it into the front of the beak to fix it more firmly.

1 Fold a large piece of thin card in half, along its shortest side. With the folded edge at the top, draw a beak shape on one side. Cut out the beak, except at the top where the card is folded.

2 Where the beak curves, use masking tape to join the two pieces of card. Snip and fold the masking tape slightly so that it lies flat and gives the beak a smooth curve.

3 Cut a 7.5 cm (3 in) slit into the top fold of the mask. On each side, fold the cardboard outwards slightly, to form two flaps. Put the mask to your face to work out where you need eyeholes to be. Cut them out. Paint the beak.

4 Cut out two oval eyes from card. Paint a large, dark pupil in each, and cut a hole in the centre. Stick these to the beak so that the eyeholes line up. Cut a strip of strong card to make a **headband** (page 13). Fix the band to the top of the mask with more tape.

5 Out of some coloured paper, cut two shapes like those shown above (top). Cut eyeholes in them. Make several cuts from the straight edge of each shape to form feathery eyelashes. Use the scissor blade to **curl** them (page 10). Glue the underside of the eyeholes and stick on each side of the mask.

6 Cut some long, thin strips, also from coloured paper. Curl them as before, and fix them to the inside front of the headband so as to form a crest.

26

LION MASK

5-litre (8¾ pint) plastic bottle
Thin cardboard for ears and eyes
Strip of elastic, at least 5 cm (2 in) wide

Instead of cardboard, this fantastic lion mask is made from plastic. You can paint it any colour you want, although orange is good for a lion. Before painting the mask you will need to rub it down with sandpaper and spray it with hairspray. This makes the paint stick better.

1 Cut the bottom 5 to 7.5 cm (2 to 3 in) off the bottle, to remove the base. Lightly sandpaper the surface of the bottle.

2 With scissors, cut strips up from the bottom, all the way around. The cuts should all end at the top of the bottle, where the sides start to curve in towards the handle and spout. With the scissor blades, **curl** all the strips outwards (page 10).

3 Position the mask in front of your face and work out where you will need eyeholes to be. Cut them either side of the handle, by carefully piercing holes with the scissor points. Cut slots where ear tabs can be inserted.

4 Cut two ears out of card, each with tabs that can be slotted into the mask and taped on the inside. Cut a diamond for a nose. Make it long enough to cover the length of the handle. Bend down the end. Make two eyes – each with eyeholes. Paint them. Stick these on to the mask or slot them in.

5 Make a hole on each side of the mask. Take a length of elastic to make a band that will fit snugly around your head. Tie the elastic to each side of the mask.

PAPER PLATE CAT

Paper plate
Thin cardboard for a nose
Elastic or string

What could be easier than using a paper plate to make a mask? As well as painting directly on to the plate, you can cover it with scraps of material to create different textures. Use glue to stick on eyes and noses. Old shoelaces or pieces of string make good whiskers – or paint them on.

1 Cut a rectangle out of the top of the plate, to make the cat's ears.

2 Cut out eyeholes. Paint the cat's face. Make a simple **nose** with card support (page 12). Colour it and glue it to the plate. Attach elastic so that the mask will stay on your face.

BEARDED FACE

Large brown envelope
Elastic or string

Envelopes and paperbags are good for making simple masks – and are quickly transformed with a touch of paint or felt-tipped pens. Instead of drawing a face, you could cut out a picture from a magazine and glue that to the front of your envelope.

1 Holding the envelope with the open end down, cut eyeholes. Fold the envelope in half lengthways. Draw half a nose and half a mouth. With the envelope folded, cut out the mouth and along the lines of the nose, leaving it as a flap.

2 For the beard, cut strips up from the bottom of the envelope to just below the mouth. Use the scissors to **curl** the strips, one thickness of paper at a time (page 10).

28

3 Colour the face. Fix elastic or string to the top corners so that it fits securely around your head.

ELEPHANT MASK

Medium-sized rectangular cardboard box
Large pieces of cardboard
Small pieces of thin card

This baby elephant mask is really easy to make from a cardboard box, with a few added features made from flat card. Use a large cereal or cardboard box depending on the size of your head!

1 With the open end of the box at the bottom, draw curves on the two widest sides. They should reach no more than a third of the way up the box. Cut them both out.

2 For the trunk, cut out a strip of card that is the same width as one of the uncut sides of the box. Curl it upwards at the end, like a trunk, and tape it to the front of the mask.

3 Cut out two large ears with tabs on them so that you can slot them into the sides of the head. Cut out two tusks and a tuft of hair. Paint all of these and leave to dry. Paint the box and leave it to dry.

4 Make eyeholes. Cut slots for ear tabs. Fold the tabs over on the inside, and tape them down. Glue the tusks to the sides of the box, pointing forwards, and stick the tuft of hair in place.

Green Fact: Many paper- and card-based products, such as toilet rolls, magazines, and cereal packets, can be made using recycled material, but only about 30% of all the paper products we buy are made this way.

29

BUFFALO BILL HAT

Pieces of corrugated cardboard or a
    cardboard box
Aluminium foil or buttons, paper and
    thin cardboard for decorations

Make this Buffalo Bill hat – or transform it
into a halo or a sombrero. Create a
Madame Butterfly wig by adding paper
butterflies and card sticks.

1 If using a cardboard box, open it out flat.
Draw and cut out your hat.

2 Paint and decorate. Make a wide
headband (page 13). Glue the flat hat to
it and leave it to dry.

30

DAGGER THROUGH THE HEAD

Wire coat hanger
Thick cardboard

Ask an adult to help you bend the coat hanger around your head and to snap off the hook. This dagger is really not difficult to make, and is sure to raise a laugh when you walk into a room! You can also adapt the idea to make a pair of big ears.

1 Draw and cut out of cardboard a dagger handle with a bit of the blade showing, and a dagger blade with a point. Paint the handle and the blade. Paint the other side too, if you like.

2 Squash a thin, wire coat hanger and then bend it so that it fits the shape of your head – over the top from ear to ear. Next, break the hook off. Do this by bending it backwards and forwards until it snaps. You should ask an adult to help you.

3 Wind tape around the wire, especially where the hook was broken off. Make sure it is a tight, but comfortable, fit around your head. Tape your blade and handle firmly to the front of the coat-hanger headband.

Create funny accessories to go with your outfit. Make spectacles from flat cardboard, noses from empty yoghurt cartons or ping-pong balls, beaks from egg boxes, and beards from envelopes. Use cardboard tubes for some crazy x-ray glasses or coloured raffia for hippy hairpieces.

MERMAID FANCY DRESS

Large cardboard box that is taller and
    wider than you when opened out
Bottle tops or aluminium foil
String

Swish a sparkling, fishy tail in this full-
length mermaid's costume. It's very easy
to make and the drawings above will give
you more ideas for fancy-dress costumes.
Collect useful scraps to make your
costume: pieces of furry fabric for a
reindeer, a tie for the pin-striped gent, or
leather strips for a cowboy's tassels.

1 Open a large cardboard box out flat. Lie down on it and, with a pen, mark where the top of your head comes. Also mark where your shoulders, waist and feet are. You might need a friend to help.

2 Using the marks you have made as a guide, draw an oval for your face to look through. Then draw the character you want to be. For the mermaid, you may need to tape on a separate piece of card for the tail.

3 Cut out your figure. If making the mermaid, take care with the tail!

4 Paint and decorate it with buttons, fabric from old clothes, beads, and ribbons. For the mermaid's scales, use aluminium foil, bottle tops or shells.

5 With closed scissors, punch two holes on either side of your figure where your arms will be. Knot the string to make arm straps. Attach further string ties as needed.

Green Fact: Many things made from aluminium foil, such as carton tops and baking and freezing trays, can be recycled. Every year thousands of tonnes of aluminium foil packaging worth a great deal of money is wasted.

ASTRONAUT'S OUTFIT

Aluminium foil and 2 foil dishes
Coloured and white paper
Cardboard: 2 long strips, approx 7.5 cm (3 in) wide;
    1 piece approx 30 x 35 cm (12 x 14 in)
Cardboard box that will fit over your head
Plastic bottles: 2 large and 3 small
Washing-up liquid bottle
Drinking straw
String
Wire from an old coat hanger

Here's everything you need for a journey through space. Draw lots of stars and planets to decorate your outfit.

Oxygen Tanks

1 Cross the strips of cardboard over your shoulders and tape them securely at the points at which they cross, both at the front and back. Cut the ends at waist level. Remove and paint them grey.

Space Shoes

1 In the middle of one of the short ends of each aluminium dish cut a slit to the base. Turn both of the dishes upside down.

2 Cut away about a third of the base of each dish – the gap should be large enough for your ankles to fit in. Cut out and colour two planets from plain paper. Glue them to the top of your shoes.

2 Decorate two large plastic bottles with foil and coloured paper. Glue them, side-by-side, to a piece of cardboard. Tape the oxygen tank to the point where the strips cross your back.

3 Tape a couple of small plastic bottles – for storing surface samples – to the front straps. Make a hole in another and stick in a straw to make a drinking bottle.

4 Tie string to the ends of the card strips at your waist, so that you can attach the whole unit securely.

Helmet

1 Draw a circle to see through at the front of the box. Cut it out. Paint your helmet and leave to dry.

2 Decorate the edges of the box with strips of aluminium foil. Draw a large planet on paper and stick it to the side of the helmet.

3 Cover an empty washing-up liquid bottle with paper. Use wire from an old coat hanger to make a square aerial. Decorate with aluminium foil. Tape the bottle to the side of the helmet.

Small figures are great fun to make and well worth spending a bit of time on. When designing rockers, be sure to include hinged parts to the characters to make them more interesting. Two people in a boat, a nodding bird, a cat at sea and a rocking horse are some of the ideas to try.

KNIGHT ON HORSEBACK ROCKER
Cereal box
2 paper plates
Plain white paper
Toilet-roll tube
Stud paper-fasteners

Add finishing touches to your rocker, such as a plume for the knight's helmet and some drinking-straw reins.

36

RECYCLE:
Cardboard boxes
Thick and thin cardboard
Toilet-roll tubes
Paper plates
Plain white paper
Stud paper-fasteners
Paper baking cases
Drinking straws

String or wool
Thin plastic bags
Fabric, ribbons, sequins, aluminium foil
Beads
Patterned wallpaper
Cotton wool or old scouring pads
Coin

1 Cut off one of the short ends of a cereal box about 5 cm (2 in) from the end. Cut a paper plate in half.

2 Tape the plate halves to each of the long sides of the box end. Tape on the inside and the outside edges. It doesn't matter if the plate is a little too long or too short.

3 About 7.5 cm (3 in) in from one of the long sides of the discarded cereal box, draw a line which steps in and out. Do this on both sides of the box, and cut it out. This will be the horse's cloak.

4 Draw a horse's head and tail on a plate. Draw the horse's head so that the ridges of the plate become its mane. Give the head and tail "stalks" for slotting into the body. Draw a pointed-crown shape for a visor. Cut these out.

5 Draw and cut out arms and legs for the knight and a circle for a helmet out of plain paper or card.

6 Paint the rocker, the toilet-roll tube and all the pieces you have cut out. Leave to dry.

7 Using double-sided or rolled tape, attach the cloak to the rocker. Cut slots for the head and tail and push them through, taping them on the inside.

8 Take the circle of card and cut a line from the edge to the centre. Fold the circle into a cone shape for a helmet, and tape firmly on the inside. Bend the visor in half, to form a point. Stick the helmet to the top of the roll and the visor just below your knight's eyes.

9 Taking care, use scissor points to make holes through the cloak and rocker. With stud paper-fasteners, fix the arms to the sides of the toilet-roll tube and the legs to the cloak. Tape the knight's body to the horse.

Green Fact: The largest rubbish dump in the world is New York City's 3,000 acre "landfill" site on Staten Island. Every month, enough rubbish to fill the Empire State Building is added to the stinking mounds. By the year 2000 the site will be completely full.

HANGING ACROBATS

4 toilet-roll tubes
Thin cardboard
Paper baking cases
Drinking straw
String or wool

Collect a few toilet-roll tubes and then it is incredibly easy to construct one of these funny mobiles to hang up in front of a window or from the middle of the ceiling.

1 Paint each toilet-roll tube with the outfit of your character.

2 On thin card draw a head, and four strips (for arms and legs) for each character. Paint these and cut them out.

3 Tape the heads to each roll. For the female acrobats' skirts, cut the centre from baking cases and slip them over the rolls. Tape in place.

4 Cut a length of drinking straw about 8 cm (3 in) long. Thread a short length of string through it and tie the ends together. Stick the hands of one of your characters over the trapeze bar. Then join together the hands and feet of the other characters.

PARACHUTISTS

Thin cardboard
Thin plastic bag

String
Small coin

Have fun dropping these parachuting people from a high window, and watch them swoop gently to the ground. Hold the plastic bag open a little to catch as much air as possible.

As far as possible make the right and left sides of your figures mirror each other. This will balance them, and they should fall smoothly when dropped. If they are not balanced, they may start spiralling and fall less well. When you draw your parachutists, make the hands and feet (or paws) wide apart, so that they look as though they are doing star jumps.

1 Draw your figure on thin card, with its arms up in the air. Paint and cut out.

2 Cut any handles off your plastic bag so that you have about 15 cm (6 in) of the bag base. Cut eight small pieces of tape and stick them close to the edges of the bag, all the way around. Snip a small hole in the middle of each piece of tape.

3 Cut eight equal-length pieces of string. Thread the ends through the reinforced holes in the bag and tape on the inside. Tape four strings from one side of the bag to the back of one hand and the other four to the back of the other. Tape a small coin to the back of the figure as a weight.

STRONG MAN
ON A STRING PULL

Thin cardboard
Stud paper-fasteners
Scrap of material
String
Bead

The joints of this strong man are linked so that he can be hung on the wall and moved by pulling the string. Adding a leopard-skin costume adds an extra touch of fun.

1 Draw and cut out the pieces of your character's body. Take care to draw each leg as one shape rather than as an upper and lower leg. Decorate and fix the pieces together with stud paper-fasteners.

2 With the back of the figure facing you, run a piece of string from the top of one arm to the top of the other arm. Do the same with a piece of string from the top of one leg to the top of the other. Tape the strings in place.

Green Fact: As well as being unsightly, litter can injure wildlife, block streams, and pollute both land and water. Birds can choke on plastic waste, and small mammals often get trapped in discarded containers.

3 Tie a long piece of string down the middle. Tie it at the top to the piece of string linking the arms, then knot it to the string linking the legs, and then let it hang down.

4 Loop a small piece of string and tape it to the back of the head so that you can hang your figure up.

5 Tie a bead or even a small piece of card to the end of the pull string. When you pull it, the arms will go up and down.

Look at the drawings above and create a string-pull character of your own. Try to draw your character's arms, legs, paws and wings opposite each other. For example, if you make the horse draw the tail opposite the front hooves. If you don't, the limbs may rise unevenly when you pull the string. Follow the step-by-step diagrams on the opposite page carefully, so that you fix the string correctly. Thread a bead on the long end of the string and it will look neatly finished.

Here is a template for the City Slicker. In pencil, draw around the shapes on to tracing paper and transfer them on to card.

CITY SLICKER

Thin cardboard
Stud paper-fasteners
String

When this hinged figure is completed, you can either attach a card stick to the back or string, which will make the limbs move when you pull it.

1 Draw a head and body, two arms with hands, two upper legs and two lower legs with feet. Cut out the pieces.

2 Paint all the parts.

3 With the scissor points, carefully make holes at the joints for your stud paper-fasteners. Fix the limbs together.

4 If you make the holes larger, so that the joints are looser, you could attach a card stick to the back of your figure and make it dance.

SEE-SAW COUPLE

2 toilet-roll tubes
Plain white paper
Thin cardboard
Stud paper-fasteners
Patterned wallpaper or similar
Cotton wool or old scouring pads
Ribbon

It's easy to make this hip-swinging couple and it should certainly take no more than a morning.

1 Stick white paper around both toilet-roll tubes. Paint faces and clothes on to each. The legs come later, so if you are painting trousers, just paint from the waistband to the tops of the legs.

2 Cut out a triangle of card for a nose. Paint it. Fold it in half and glue it on to the face.

3 Decorate your figures. Cut out a paper tie, buttons and a belt. For a skirt, draw around a mug on to patterned paper. Cut it out. In the centre, draw around the end of a toilet-roll tube. Cut the centre out. Slip the skirt on your figure and tape it.

4 Draw arms and legs for each character on to card. All the strips should be the same length, but put feet on the legs. Paint these to match the characters' clothing on the toilet-roll tube bodies.

5 With scissor points, carefully make a hole in the top of each of the arms and legs. Also make holes in the sides of the tubes where you want the arms and legs to go.

47

6 Fasten the arms and legs to the bodies. When you have two figures, make holes in their feet and hands and join each hand and foot to the opposite hand and foot on the other figure.

7 Make hair out of cotton wool. Add ribbons if you like. Glue this to the top of the figures.

Collect different bits and pieces to make hair and accessories for your characters.

Treasure Island Game

This is a game of thrills and excitement as players face pirates, sharks and crocodiles in their search for lost treasure. It takes a little time to make the map and all the different pieces and wait for them to dry, but once made this is a game that can be enjoyed again and again.

RECYCLE:

For the Board
Newspaper
White sheet
Thin cardboard

Extra item: a sponge

For the Palm Trees
Thin cardboard

For the Pirate Flags
Plain white paper
Drinking straw

For the Treasure Chest
Small box
Plain white paper
String

1 Spread out some newspaper before starting. Put the sheet on top. Firstly in pencil, and then with a thin black marker pen, draw 17 islands of different sizes on it.

2 Paint in the sea around the islands. Use water on your brush to thin the colour in some places.

3 Paint in the islands. Once dry, you can draw around the edges again with a thicker black pen. You can also paint on compass points at the near end of the sheet.

4 Draw a crocodile shape on to card. Cut it out from the middle, so that it can be used as a template.

5 Using a sponge dipped in green paint (and squeezed out), use the template to stencil about 12 crocodiles on to the sea and islands. When dry, paint white eyes and teeth on to your crocodiles, and then draw around these with a black pen.

6 Draw a shark's fin on to card. Cut it out from the middle to make another template. You could draw a fish template too, if you like.

49

7 Use a sponge dipped in dark-blue paint to stencil sharks' fins on to the sheet. Paint about 20, but put several together in small groups. When dry, paint white lines under the fins so that they look as if they are coming out of the water.

8 With a thin black pen, divide up the sheet into equal sections. Make sure you have at least six sections along the bottom and nine up the side. You can have more, but make sure that the squares you draw are not smaller than the pirate ships.

PALM TREES

TREASURE CHEST

1 Paint a small box brown. Cut out two long strips of paper and paint them a darker brown. When dry, glue one around each end of the box.

2 Paint and cut out a lock with a hole in it. Tie the string through the lock and around the middle of the box.

1 Draw 15 palm trees and bases on plain card. Paint and cut them out.

2 Fold over the bottom of the tree trunks and tape them to the bases so that they stand upright. Stand them on the islands. Mark each palm tree base with points from 1 to 4, so that small islands have a score of 3 or 4, and bigger ones a score of 1 or 2.

PIRATE FLAGS FOR ISLANDS AND SHIPS

HOW TO PLAY

Pieces for the Game:

15 palm trees, one treasure chest, pirate ships for each player, two pirate islands, a large coin.

Setting Up the Game:

1. Spread out the sheet.
2. Put the treasure chest on a distant island.
3. Put out the palm trees, with the higher scoring ones on the small islands and the lower scoring ones on the large islands.
4. Stand your pirate flags on two of the islands to make them pirate islands.

Playing the Game:

The aim of each player is for their pirate ship to be the first to reach the treasure. Stand at the bottom of the sheet.

Taking it in turns, the first player throws the coin, aiming for it to land on an island with a high score. Whatever score is gained, the player moves his or her pirate ship that number of spaces on the sheet. Moves can be made forwards, backwards, sideways or diagonally.

If the coin lands touching a crocodile, you miss a go; if it lands touching a shark, you move back one space; and if it lands on a pirate island you have to go back to the beginning!

1 Draw a skull and crossbones on to paper. Paint the background black, and fix it to a short length of drinking straw.

2 Paint the matchboxes different colours for each player. Make a hole in the top of each and push the straw flags in. Glue if necessary. Also cut out bases and stick on flags to make two pirate islands.

Marble Runs

You don't need lots of bits and pieces to make marble runs and they can be as simple or as complicated as you like. Once made, you can play the Jousting Game with friends. The Helter-Skelter and Step-by-Step runs are fun to make for younger brothers and sisters.

RECYCLE:

Cardboard box
Thick and thin cardboard
Corrugated cardboard
Toilet-roll tubes
Plain white paper
Used matches or cocktail sticks
Corks
Marbles
Cardboard tube
Pull-off cap from a canister
Marble
Matchboxes or other small boxes

JOUSTING GAME

Low-sided box
Thin card
Corrugated cardboard
6 toilet-roll tubes
Paper
Used matches or cocktail sticks
5 corks
Marbles

In this game, you have to get past five brave knights and enter the jousting tents. Decorate the knights so their colours match those of the tents they protect.

1 If you don't have a low-sided box, cut one down from an ordinary box. Make sure the sides are no more than 7.5 cm (3 in) high.

2 Cut a strip of card a little narrower than the height of the box, but as wide as one of the shorter ends. Glue the strip in place.

3 Cut a large piece of card the same size as the base of the box. Position this in the box, resting it at one end on the glued-in strip, so that it forms a gentle slope.

5 Take five toilet-roll tubes and cut doors – 3 cm (1¼ in) high, and wide enough for a marble to fit through – at the front and back of each of them. Paint them different colours.

6 Make roofs for the tents. Draw around a mug on to paper. Cut out five circles. Cut a single slit from the edge to the centre of each one. Make each into a cone shape and tape to secure. Paint to match the colours of the tents.

54

4 Paint the whole thing with stripes of green to look like freshly cut grass.

Green Fact: Cutting down trees is harmful to the environment. Trees help keep the Earth cool, and soak up the poisonous gas carbon dioxide, which contributes to the Greenhouse Effect.

7 Draw five flags and number them. Paint and cut them out. Stick each to a used match or cocktail stick. Snip a tiny hole in the top of each roof and glue the flags in.

8 Glue the tents next to each other at the bottom of the sloping end of the box, with a door facing the front.

9 Cut five strips of corrugated cardboard 3 cm (1¼ in) high and 10 cm (4 in) long. Paint them green. When dry, bend into "V" shapes and stick them between the jousting tents to make fences. Cut one strip in half and stick on each side of the box.

10 To make the knights, paint five corks grey. Leave space to paint on pink faces. Add visors.

11 Make plumes for the knights. Cut leaf shapes out of paper. Cut thin strips all around them. **Curl** each strip using scissor blades (page 10). Glue the plumes into the holes left by a corkscrew in the top of each cork. (You may need to make these bigger using the point of a pencil.)

12 Glue the knights in a row, about 9 cm (3½ in) in front of the opening of each tent. If you want to make the game harder, make one extra knight and glue him in the middle of the board, in front of the entrance to the tower.

13 Make a tower from which to release your marbles. Cut a door out of one end of a toilet-roll tube. It must be wide enough for the marble to get through. Cut notches all around the top. Glue the tower on the board at the opposite end from the jousting tents.

55

HOW TO PLAY

Each player takes it in turn to drop his or her marbles down the tower. The marbles will roll past the knights into the jousting tents, scoring points from 1 to 5. Add up all the points, then let the next person have a go. Vary the rules so the winner is the person who scores the lowest points! Or award bonus points for reaching the same tent twice in a row. You could choose a tent to be a booby tent that scores no points.

HELTER-SKELTER

Large cardboard tube
Thick and thin cardboard
Pull-off cap from a canister
Marble

You might have to ask at a stationer's
for an empty tube large enough to
make the helter-skelter from.

*Get a grown-up to ask at a local furniture store or
carpet shop for part of a cardboard tube from
inside a roll of carpet. Then you can make a huge
helter-skelter!*

STEP-BY-STEP

Large matchboxes or small
boxes
Thick cardboard

This marble run can be
made from any small
boxes – as long as they
are all the same size.

1 Cut good-sized, rectangular holes in each
box. Make one hole at the top of each
box and another at the opposite end at the
bottom. Each hole should be big enough for a
marble to fall through easily.

1 Place the tube on thick card from the side of a box, and cut out a circle. Tape this to the top. Draw around your tube about eight more times.

2 Using the circles you have drawn as a starting point, draw curls on the card. Each should be 3 cm (1¼ in) wide, narrowing to 2.5 cm (1 in) at one end. Cut them out.

3 Using plenty of masking tape, fix the first curl securely to the side of the tube. Spiral it gently downwards as you tape it. When the first curl is attached, start the next one about 4.5 cm (1¾ in) further down the tube. Make sure the first curl overhangs the start of the second curl by about 2 cm (¾ in).

4 Continue fixing the curls until you are about 7.5 cm (3 in) from the bottom. Cut several strips of ordinary cardboard 2 cm (¾ in) wide and about 12 cm (4¾ in) long. These are to form the outside edges of the chutes. Tape them securely to the sides.

5 Take the cap off a canister and turn it upside down for a cup. Tape this below the end of the final chute, to catch the marble.

6 Before painting the helter-skelter, try rolling your marble from the top. You may need to make adjustments to the angle of the chutes to make them run smooth. When you are happy, add any final masking tape and then paint.

57

2 Lie the boxes on their sides, one above the other to form steps. The hole in the bottom of one box should be positioned above the hole in the top of the next box. Tape all the boxes together like this.

3 Lay the stepped boxes across the middle of a large square of strong card. Draw around the edge of each box. Cut along the zig-zag you have drawn, to make a triangle of card with the zig-zag on one side.

4 Paint the marble run. From the remaining cardboard, make a triangular stand and fix it to the back so your marble run stands up.

Octopus Hoopla

You can play Octopus Hoopla as a scoring game, where the winner is the first player to score fifty, or as a game of skill, where players must hoop from one to eight in that order. Swap turns after every five goes.

RECYCLE:

Cardboard box
Plain paper
String

Extra items: a plate, a sponge

Instead of using an octopus for the hoopla game, you could make a dog, a tree with lots of branches or a funny face.

1 Open out a large cardboard box and draw an octopus on it. Don't forget that an octopus has eight legs!

2 Cut out the octopus. Bend the legs up to make hooks for the hoops to be thrown over. Tape them in their bent positions.

3 Paint both sides of your octopus in a single colour. When dry, add eyes and a smile. Draw or paint on spots to look like suckers. In another shade or colour, sponge patches of paint over the legs. Leave to dry.

4 To make the hoops, draw around a plate on to card. Draw another circle about 2.5 cm (1 in) in from the outer one. Cut out each circle and their middles to make hoops and then paint them.

5 On paper, paint numbers from 1 to 8 in circles. Stick them on to the legs from left to right.

6 Tape a loop of string behind the octopus' head so that it can be hung on the wall. Make sure the legs are bent forward.

59

Skittles

Here are two kinds of skittles for you to make.
The monster skittles can be quite big and heavy
and are great for playing with outdoors.
Swing skittles are best to play with
indoors where the wind won't blow
them over.

MONSTER SKITTLES

Plastic bottles
Plain white paper
Thin cardboard
Tube caps
    Bottle tops
     Cardboard eggboxes
     Wool or string
    Sand, soil or salt

Make a scary one-eyed
monster or a hairy troll.

RECYCLE:

Plastic bottles
Plain white paper
Thin cardboard
Caps off tubes and plastic bottle tops
Cardboard eggboxes
Wool

String
Toilet-roll tubes
Cardboard box
Newspaper
Aluminium foil

Extra items: sand, soil or salt

1 Find plastic bottles the same size and tape a piece of plain paper around each of them.

2 Draw a monster face on to the paper, and paint it.

3 On thin card draw and cut out extra features such as hands or claws, feet and bulging eyes.

4 Glue these pieces on, or carefully cut slits in the sides of the bottle, and slot them in. Don't cut any slits lower than about 7.5 cm (3 in) from the bottom of the bottle.

5 Make warts for the monsters out of tube caps, bottle tops and bits of eggboxes, and glue them in place. Paint them.

6 To make a hairy monster, wrap wool loosely around your fingers. Take the loop off and, with a separate piece of wool, tie it at one end. Cut through the strands at the other end to make a tuft. Push this through the slits.

61

7 Put some sand, soil or salt into the bottles up to about 7.5 cm (3 in) from the bottom and replace the tops. Weighting the skittles makes them harder to knock down. Use a tennis ball and try!

SWING SKITTLES

Toilet-roll tubes
Thin cardboard
Plain white paper
Cardboard box
Newspaper
Aluminium foil
String

To play swing skittles, put the swing ball in the stand. Place all the skittles on the base. Swing the ball out and try to knock down as many skittles in one go as you can. See how many goes it takes to knock them all down.

Instead of soldiers, you could have a field of pirates, cowboys or aliens!

1 Make the skittles from toilet-roll tubes. Paint each one, making the top third the face and the bottom two-thirds the body. To make soldiers, add features like a moustache.

2 Cut a small triangle out of card to make a nose, and paint it the same colour as the face. When it is dry, fold it into a point and glue it on the tube.

3 Draw a hat on a piece of card. Make the brim wider than the cardboard tube. Cut it out and paint it. Cut a hat decoration out of paper. Paint the decoration and glue it to the hat. Cut slots on either side of the tube and slot the hat into place.

Green Fact: Many newspapers are now made from recycled paper. This is good news for Australia's eucalyptus trees, which are chopped down to make woodchips that in turn make paper pulp.

4 To make a rectangular base for the skittles, open out a cardboard box and cut off one side with its flaps.

5 Cut a length of cardboard about 20 cm (10 in) long. Cut strips at one end about 5 cm (2 in) in length. Push these out to form a stand. Cut a hole in the middle of the long edge of your skittle base. Push the tube through and tape it to the underside of the base.

63

6 Make a pole by rolling up some sheets of newspaper neatly and tightly. Fix it with tape. It should be made fat and firm enough to stand securely upright in the tubing stand. Paint it and leave to dry.

7 Make a ball out of newspaper and tape it to a piece of string. Cut the string so that when it is fixed to the top of the pole the ball at the other end hangs just above the base.

Mini Games

Victorian children used to play with wooden toys, but these mini games are made from plastic and paper. Decorate a large yoghurt carton for the throw-and-catch pot and paint brightly coloured circles or funny characters on the spinner.

RECYCLE:
Plain white paper
Yoghurt carton
String
Newspaper
Thick cardboard

Extra item: a small plate

THROW-AND-CATCH POT

Plain white paper
Large yoghurt carton
String approx. 25.5 cm (10 in) long
Newspaper

Hold the pot with the ball hanging outside on its string. The aim of the game is to flick the ball upwards and into the pot.

1 Wrap a piece of paper around the yoghurt carton. On the paper, mark where the top and bottom of the pot fall, and where the paper overlaps so that it can be cut and taped to fit the pot neatly. Paint it.

2 With scissors, carefully make a hole in the bottom of the carton. To help prevent it from cracking, you could cover the bottom with masking tape before puncturing it.

SPINNER
Thick cardboard
String

Draw around a small plate or a mug to get nice even circles. Paint on a twirling figure or circles, or both!

1 Cut out two circles from card, about 10 cm (4 in) in diameter. Paint them on both sides. When dry, make two small holes near the centre of each disc.

These simple toys are good ones to start with. Then you can move on to bigger toy-making projects.

2 Thread the string through two holes and back through the other two. Knot the string. Put your fingers into the loop on each side and twirl it away from you to twist the string. When you can twist no further, pull the string tight and the disc will spin.

Green Fact: A lot of the food we buy comes wrapped in plastic. Try and re-use plastic containers whenever you can: put sandwiches in a margarine tub instead of wrapping them in clingfilm.

3 Thread a piece of string through the hole and tape the end to the base. Make a ball out of newspaper. Tape it and paint it. When dry, attach it securely to the other end of the string with some more tape. Paint it to match.

Tin-Can Games

Recycle old tin cans in a completely new way: next time you finish a can of beans, wash it out and find another one the same size to make a telephone! Empty paint tins make great stilts because they're solid and difficult to fall off.

RECYCLE:

Tin cans
String
Paint tins
Cord or string
Plain white paper

Extra items: a hammer and nail

TELEPHONE

2 tin cans, the same size, with their labels on
Long piece of smooth string

Keep the string taut and you'll be able to speak to a friend from several metres away.

You'll need an adult's help with the hammer and nail. And remember – never use a rusty tin can!

1 With the help of an adult, make a small hole in the bottom of each tin with the hammer and nail.

2 Thread a long piece of string through the cans, tying a firm knot at each end so that it will not slip back through the hole.

3 Decorate each tin. Standing at opposite ends of a room and, keeping the string taut between you, whisper into your tin while a friend has the other tin to his or her ear. Try talking and even singing.

STILTS

2 large paint tins, the same size,
    with handles
Cord or thick string
Plain white paper

Use empty paint tins. Leave the lids
off for any remaining paint to dry,
then replace the lids.

1 Tie cord or thick string to one side of the
handle, where it meets the tin.

67

2 Stand on the tin to see at what height you
will want to hold the cord. Cut the cord
and tie it to the other side of the tin.

3 Wrap paper around the tins and tape it.
Decorate the tins with whatever pattern
you like.

Fishing Game

You can hook these fish out of a cardboard box or off the ground. Time yourself and see how many points you can score in five minutes. Or make a second rod and have a fishing competition with a friend. Start together and see who has the highest score at the end of the contest.

1 Draw fish of three different sizes on to thin cardboard. The largest fish are worth 1 point, the middle-sized fish are worth 3 points and the smallest fish are worth 5 points. Cut them out.

RECYCLE:

Thin cardboard
Paperclips
Newspaper
String approx. 45 cm (18 in) long

2 Paint the fish different colours. When they are dry, paint on scales, a mouth and eyes in other colours.

3 Tape paperclips on the back of the fish at the nose end, so that the clip sticks well out beyond the cardboard on the big fish, a little less on the medium-sized fish and hardly at all on the smallest fish. This makes the small ones the hardest to catch.

4 Make a rod by tightly rolling up a couple of sheets of newspaper and taping it securely. Paint it.

5 Tie one end of the string to a paperclip. Carefully open up the paperclip to make a hook. Attach the other end of the string to the newspaper rod.

Green Fact: An accidental victim of the fishing industry is the dolphin. Dolphins breathe air and, if they become entangled in the nets put out to catch tuna, they can suffocate.

Transport

With a big cardboard box and some other odds and ends you can fight an aerial battle, compete in a race or brave the oceans in your very own fishing boat. A twisted length of strong fabric or a pair of old tights knotted inside the body of the plane, car or boat make good carrying straps. You might need a grown-up to help you while you check that the length of the straps is right for your height.

RECYCLE:

Cardboard boxes
Thick and thin cardboard
Kitchen-roll tubes
Toilet-roll tubes
Newspaper
Aluminium foil
Jar lids
Drinking straws
String
Plain white paper
Yoghurt cartons

Extra items:

Small plate
Length of cane
Fabric or tights

1 Tape down all the sides to the box so that it is secure. Towards the back of the box cut a hole through the top and bottom, big enough for you to stand in. This is the cockpit. You could fix a second box to the front if you want your plane to be longer. Paint it.

2 On cardboard, draw a tailpiece with an extension that can be bent inwards to attach the tailpiece to the body of the plane. Cut it out. Draw around this and cut out a second tailpiece. Bend in the flaps and tape the tailpiece to the back of the cockpit. Tape the tail fins together. Paint them.

3 Draw and cut out a wing in the shape shown above. Use this as a template to cut out three more. This is a bi-plane and has two wings on each side.

4 To support and strengthen the wings glue or tape three kitchen-roll tubes of equal length between two wings. You can also make your own tubes out of newspaper, thickly and tightly rolled. Paint each double wing.

PLANE

Large, rectangular cardboard box
Thick and thin cardboard
6 kitchen-roll tubes or
    newspaper
2 toilet-roll tubes
Small plate

Aluminium foil
Jar lid
Cane or strip of wood
String
Fabric or tights

Be a flying ace in
this bi-plane.

You can adapt this idea for a plane and turn it into a steam train or a rocket.

5 Draw around a small plate twice on to card. Cut these circles out. Cut slots in the ends of two toilet-roll tubes and fold them outwards. Tape them under the plane. Tape the card circles to the sides of the tubes, at the bottom, to look like tyres.

6 Cut out a wide semi-circle of card for a windscreen. Paint it and draw on some windscreen wipers. Cut slots at the bottom to make it easier to bend the screen gently into a curve. Use masking tape to fix the screen inside the front of the cockpit.

7 Draw a large propeller on to card. Cut it out. Spread glue over one side and lay it on to aluminium foil. When dry, cut around the foil – leaving some overlap. Cut notches in it, fold it around the edges and tape it down. Glue a large jar lid to the centre.

8 Tape the back of the propeller to a cane or rounded stick of wood. Make a hole in the front of the plane. Push the cane through so that you can turn the propeller from the inside of the plane.

9 To make the plane easier to store, the wings are detachable. Hold them up to the body of the plane. Mark with a pencil where the top wing overlaps the cockpit and where the first tube support meets the side. Make holes in the body and the wing and thread through string to fix them together.

10 To make shoulder straps twist strips of strong fabric and knot them through holes made in the side of your plane. Make sure they are the right length for your height.

CAR

Large, rectangular cardboard box
Thick cardboard
Drinking straws
Aluminium foil
Newspaper
2 yoghurt cartons
Small plate
4 jar lids
Fabric or tights

Before painting the yoghurt cartons, rub them down with sandpaper. When decorated, fix the paint by spraying on pump-action hairspray.

If you don't have jar lids, make hubcaps out of card.

1 Cut off the base of your box. At the top, towards one end, cut a hole big enough for you to fit in easily. Draw a curve, as shown, on both sides. Cut off and discard the shaded area shown above, so that you are left with the end flap of the box.

2 Bend the end flap gently and tape it back along the curve. This makes the back of the car.

3 To make a boot, cut a flap on three sides that can be bent up.

4 Cut a piece of card that fits the space between the cockpit and the boot of the car. Tape it in place. Paint the car and leave it to dry.

5 Cut out a semi-circle of card and tape drinking straws to it. Glue aluminium foil loosely over the whole thing. Gently press the foil around the straws so that it takes on the shape of a radiator grill. Cover two fat rolls of newspaper in foil to make bumpers. Make number plates with your name on.

6 Fix all the pieces to the car. Paint two large yoghurt cartons yellow on the inside and the same colour as your car on the outside. When dry, tape over the middle of the cartons to fix them to the top of the front of the car.

7 Cut out a semi-circle of card for a windscreen. Cut little slots all along the bottom edge. Paint the windscreen and add wipers. When dry, fold up the tabs and tape them inside the car, gently bending the windscreen to fit the curve of the cockpit.

8 On thick card draw round a plate and cut out four card wheels. Paint them to show the tyres. Glue on jar lids for hubcaps. Glue the wheels to the sides of the car, overlapping the bottom. Make shoulder straps as described on page 70.

Green Fact: We can cut down the amount of harm done by cars by using them less. Persuade adults to walk instead of drive, and to share car space with neighbours.

When the car is not being played with, it rests on its wheels. To make them extra strong, you can use two circles of card glued together. Let them dry thoroughly then paint on tyres and hubcaps.

FISHING BOAT

Large, rectangular cardboard box
Thick cardboard
3 toilet-roll tubes
Newspaper
Aluminium foil

Plain white paper
Kitchen-roll tube
Fabric or tights

You can sit in the boat and play the fishing game on page 68.

1 Cut off one of the longest and widest sides of the box so that you can sit in it. Next cut off one of the short ends. Then cut the base of the box, to about a third of the way back along each of the long sides.

2 Gently bend the two ends in to form a point at the bow of the boat. Tape them together.

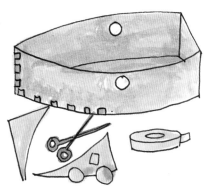

3 Cut off the cardboard left sticking out at either side of the bow of the boat. Tape the base to the curved sides of the bow. Cut out two circular holes on each side of the boat for the oars to fit through.

4 Cut out a large hole in the base of the boat so that you can stand up in it. Paint the outside of the boat and give it a name.

5 Cut a rudder out of thick cardboard, in the shape shown above. Tape the handle inside a toilet-roll tubes. Paint it. When the paint is dry, cut a slot in the stern of the boat and fit the rudder in it.

With the remaining cardboard cut out some fish shapes and cover them with aluminium foil.

6 Cut two paddle shapes out of card. Make long, strong handles by tightly rolling up sheets of newspaper. Tape the newspaper tubes and then trim the ends so that they are neat. Tape each long handle to the back of a paddle to make oars. Paint them.

7 Cut an anchor out of thick card, with a loop at the top. Spread glue on one side and stick it on a sheet of aluminium foil. Cut around the foil, about 5 cm (2 in) from the edge of the anchor. Fold the foil around the sides and tape it down.

8 Make an anchor chain by slicing up sections of two toilet-roll tubes. Cut half of the links so that they are open. Join them up with tape, to make a chain, and link one end to the loop of the anchor. Tape the other end to the stern of the boat.

9 Make a flag out of a tube of rolled newspaper and a triangle of paper. Make a flag holder out of a kitchen-roll tube and fix it inside the back of the boat. Paint the holder and the flag.

10 Make straps out of wide strips of fabric or tights. Make a couple of holes on each side of the boat and tie the straps at the right length for you to wear comfortably.

Green Fact: Life on Earth began in the oceans more than three-and-a-half billion years ago. Different oceans have different "landscapes" and populations. Australia's Great Barrier Reef is home to over 3,000 animal species.

Motorbike

You can decorate both sides of this motorbike the same way or paint them in different colours so that you have two different bikes. You might like to paint just one side, stick on half a handlebar and use the bike to decorate your bedroom. If you don't have a big enough cardboard box a large sheet of thick cardboard will do.

RECYCLE:

Large, rectangular cardboard box
Small boxes
Paint-tin lids
Jar lids
Drinking straws
Newspaper or cardboard tubing
Aluminium foil
Small plastic bottle with screw cap

Extra item: a round tray

Make spanners for your motorbike by covering cardboard shapes with aluminium foil.

79

1 Open out the cardboard box and draw the outline of a motorbike. Draw around a wastepaper bin or a round tray for the wheels.

2 Cut out the motorbike.

3 Glue small boxes and jar lids to the middle of the bike to look like mechanical parts. Add cardboard circles or lids from empty paint tins to make hubcaps.

4 Cut about 20 short lengths from drinking straws and wrap them in aluminium foil. Glue these on to the bike, around the hubcaps, to make wheel spokes.

5 To make handlebars, roll up a few sheets of newspaper and tape them together, or use a cardboard tube. With scissors, make a hole at the front of the bike just large enough for the tube to fit through it. Tape securely.

6 Cut the top off a small plastic bottle that has a screw cap. Glue the cone to the bike – this is the petrol tank and you can take the cap on and off.

7 Paint the bike. Make a long roll of newspaper tubing, and cover it in aluminium foil. Stick this to the bike as an exhaust pipe.

8 Cut out a piece of cardboard that reaches from the handlebars to the front wheel hub. Make mudguards for the front and back wheels. Paint these pieces and attach them.

Moving Toys

Elastic bands provide the power to propel the boat and the racing car, while a slip of paper and a paperclip are all you need to make a tiny yacht. Make a few of these toys and have races with your friends.

RECYCLE:

Small plastic bottle
Ball-point pens
Small box
Thin cardboard
Elastic bands
Paperclips
Plain white paper
Toilet-roll tube
Bottle tops
Drinking straws

Extra items:
sandpaper, pump-action hairspray

PADDLE BOAT

Small plastic bottle   Thin cardboard
2 ball-point pens   Elastic band
Small box

As the boat is made of plastic, you need to prepare the surface by rubbing it down with sandpaper then spraying it with hairspray. The clear varnish makes the boat waterproof.

1 Cut a strip out of one side of the bottle to form the hull of your boat. Keep the piece you cut out.

2 Tape a ball-point pen to both sides of the bottle. Half of each pen should stick out beyond the bottle base.

3 Cut a rectangle of plastic as long as the pen ends from the piece you have left from making the hull. This will be the paddle.

4 If you want to make a cabin, glue a small box into the hull.

5 Rub the plastic down with sandpaper ready to paint it. Paint the upper and lower parts of the boat different colours. Do one colour at a time so they don't smudge.

6 Draw a line of people on thin cardboard and colour them in. Cut them out and tape them into the boat so they are looking out.

Green Fact: CFCs (Chlorofluorocarbons) are gases that harm the ozone layer. They are used in the manufacture of polystyrene containers such as those in which take-away hamburgers are served.

7 Using hobby glue or clear nail varnish, glaze the whole boat.

8 Put an elastic band around both pens and put the rectangle of plastic through it. Holding the boat with the back facing you, rotate the piece of plastic. When you can't turn it any more, put it in the bath, let it go and watch it sail away.

PAPERCLIP YACHT

Paperclips
Plain white paper

These tiny yachts are great to play with in a big bowl of water. Make lots and have a boat race.

1 Bend up the inner curved end of a paperclip so that it stands straight and makes an L shape.

2 Cut out squares of paper no taller than the top of the L to make little sails. Paint them. When they are dry slip them into the paperclip and blow them across a bowl of water.

RACING CAR

Toilet-roll tube
4 metal bottle tops
Thin cardboard
2 drinking straws
Elastic band

Two drinking straws and an elastic band make this car whizz across a table top. For extra grip, wind elastic bands around the rear tyres. Make two or three cars with different colours and numbers and race them with your friends.

84

1 Cut a cockpit hole out of a toilet-roll tube. Make small holes as low down the side of the tube as possible for the axle. The wheels should keep the undercarriage off the floor.

2 Draw around four bottle tops on to card (the front and back wheels must be the same size). Make a hole in the middle of the discs for a straw to go through. Trim the card circles so they fit into the bottle tops.

3 Cut two lengths of drinking straws. Push them through the toilet-roll tube to form axles. Snip slits into all four ends.

4 Push the snipped ends through the card discs, open them out and tape them down. Push them into the bottle tops.

5 Loop an elastic band through itself around the front axle inside the tube. The elastic band should be slightly longer than the car.

6 Pull the elastic band back through the tube to the rear axle and tape it to the middle of the straw. To make the car move, wind back the axle anti-clockwise until the elastic is tight. Put the car on the ground and let it go.

7 Fill in the front of the car by drawing around the tube and cutting out the circle of card. Tape it on. Paint the car and when it is dry add numbers. If you like, make an exhaust from a piece of straw.

8 Make a little man out of card, paint him and tape him into the cockpit. Make sure he doesn't touch the elastic band.

Play House

This play house is large enough to play in or to keep toys in. You can decorate it as a country cottage, a manor house or a haunted house. Fill the window boxes with daisies, daffodils and roses.

RECYCLE:
For the House
Large cardboard box or four large pieces of flat cardboard
Thick and thin cardboard
String

For the Window Box
Shallow box
String

For the Flowers and Plant Pots
Cardboard eggboxes
Newspaper
Thin cardboard
Coloured tissue paper
Yoghurt cartons

Extra items: pump-action hairspray, sandpaper

Green Fact: Even if you live in a high-rise block you can have your own garden. To begin, all you need is a warm, sunny windowsill, some empty margarine tubs, and a few mustard and cress seeds.

1 Open up the cardboard box and arrange the sides so that you have four equal-sized panels next to each other. (You may have to cut the box into panels.) Tape the pieces together.

2 Starting from the bottom of one panel cut out two further sides to make a door. Cut out a letterbox.

3 On one or two of the other panels, cut out squares for windowpanes. Cut out four card strips the right lengths to make a frame for the complete window. Angle the ends of each strip as shown above. Glue them in place.

4 Paint the house. You could paint on bricks, a door number and grass around the base. Stand it up and leave it to dry.

5 Join the two unattached walls of the house with string. Use scissors to make four pairs of holes opposite each other. Cut four equal lengths of string. Thread these through each set of holes and tie bows.

6 To begin the roof, cut out a wide cardboard rectangle that is a little longer than one side of the house.

7 Mark the top edge, a hand's width in on each side. Draw straight lines from these marks to the bottom corners, and a wavy line along the bottom edge. Cut out the panel.

8 Trace the panel and cut out three more. Lay the short sides of the roof panels next to each other and join them with masking tape.

9 Make pairs of holes and link the unattached edges with string fastenings as for the walls. Cut a square of card to cover the hole in the middle of the roof. Make it just a little bigger than the hole.

10 Paint all the roof pieces. When they are dry, use a black marker pen to draw on roof tiles. If the walls are much taller than you are, ask an adult to help you put the roof on the house.

WINDOW BOX

1 Paint the box and leave it to dry. Make a hole at each edge in the house wall, just beneath the window frame. Attach the box to the wall with string.

2 You may need to make small card hinges to give the window box some extra support. Bend them back and tape them to the wall.

DAFFODILS

1 Draw and cut out stars from cardboard.

2 Cut out the cupped sections from a cardboard eggbox, and snip them so that they have pointed edges.

3 Glue the crown-shaped pieces of eggbox in the centre of each cardboard star. Paint them yellow.

4 Draw long, thin stems with long pointed leaves on to cardboard. Paint them. When they are dry, stick the flower heads in place.

ROSES

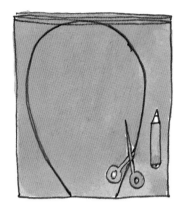

1 Paint the whole of one side of a sheet of newspaper. Leave to dry. Paint the other side, and leave that to dry too.

2 Fold the paper so that it is several layers thick, but still thin enough for you to cut through with a pair of scissors to make petals.

3 Lay a strip of masking tape, sticky side up, on a table. Stick the petals along it, in a straight line.

4 Roll up the tape, and as you roll it, pinch in the bottom, to make it look like a rose.

5 Tightly roll up sheets of newspaper and tape them closed to make stems. Paint them and, when dry, tape the rose heads to them.

Green Fact: If you have a garden, make sure it is 'green' by not using chemical pesticides and fertilisers. Recycle your vegetable peeling by starting a compost heap or a wormery – but ask a grown-up for help.

90

DAISIES

1 From thin card draw and cut out daisy shapes and stems with two small leaves.

2 Paint the pieces. Tear up small pieces of coloured tissue paper and scrunch them into balls. Stick these on to the centre of the daisy head.

PLANT POTS

1 Spray small plastic cartons with hairspray after rubbing them down with sandpaper. Paint them.

2 Turn the pots upside down and trace around them on to cardboard then cut out the circles you have drawn. Make a hole in the top of each card disc for the flower stems to go through.

3 Push the stems through the holes and glue the cardboard rounds to the tops of the yoghurt cartons.

Decorations

Make these frames and the lampshade to decorate your bedroom. They also make good presents for parents and friends.

RECYCLE:

Thin cardboard
Glue
String
Aluminium foil
Plain white paper
Greaseproof paper

Extra items: lampshade frame

SILVER FRAME

Thin cardboard
Glue
String
Aluminium foil

This picture frame has an attractive raised surface design. Cut the centre hole a little smaller than the picture you want to frame, and tape the picture to the back.

1 Decide what you want to put in the frame then use a pencil and ruler to draw the frame size you want. Cut it out of cardboard and make a hole in the middle where the picture will appear.

2 Draw a design on the border in pencil. Next, draw over this pattern in lines of glue. Cut lengths of string and lay them on top of the glue so that they stick. Let the glue dry.

3 Put glue all over the front of the frame. Place a large piece of aluminium foil over the top, pressing it around the string pattern. Cut the edges and centre of the foil then fold it round the frame and stick it down.

BUS FRAME

Thin cardboard
String

This frame holds lots of photographs. If you don't want to use photographs, cut pictures from magazines.

1 Draw a double-decker bus with several windows, a door and wheels on to card. Add a driver. Paint it red with black tyres.

2 Cut out windows – this is where the photos will go. Tape a loop of string to the back of the bus to hang it on the wall.

LAMPSHADE

Plain white paper
Greaseproof paper

This lampshade looks magical. Ask an adult to check that the shade is far enough away from the bulb that it will not catch fire.

1 Cut a piece of paper that will fit neatly around the lampshade frame. Make it about 5 cm (2 in) longer than the frame. Draw shapes all over it up to 5 cm (2 in) from the edge and cut them out.

2 Tape the greaseproof paper to the table you are working on, then paint it in patches of different colours.

3 When dry, cut squares from the grease-proof paper to cover the holes cut in the plain paper. Put glue around the edges of the holes on one side of the paper. Stick a coloured patch over each.

4 Cut slits up the 5 cm (2 in) unpatterned part of the paper, to give a tasselled effect. Tape the shade over the frame. If the light bulb hangs, put the tassels at the bottom; if it sits upright on a stand, put them at the top.

Animal Chair

Turn an ordinary wooden chair into a fabulous animal chair!
A giraffe is good to make because it is tall, but you can use
whatever animal you like. A wooden chair is best as then you
can paint the back and the legs to match the animal's markings.

RECYCLE:

2 large cardboard boxes
String
Plain white paper

Extra item: a chair

1 Open out the first box. Put it on the floor and lay your chair on its side on top of it. Draw round it.

2 Remove the chair. Using what you have just drawn as a guide, draw an animal so that the outline of the chair is inside it. Cut out the animal shape.

3 Draw around this animal on to the other opened box. Cut out this second animal. Now you have one for each side of the chair.

4 Paint the body of the giraffe and add markings, hoofs, nostils and eyes. (If you prefer, you can cut out white paper circles for eyes instead and glue them on.) Paint the chair too if you are allowed. Allow to dry.

5 Hold the animal shapes against the sides of the chair and mark where the string ties should go. Carefully pierce holes in the cardboard and use string or strips of fabric to tie the neck and legs to the chair. Stick paper on to a strip of masking tape, paint it black and snip it to make a mane and tufts for the tail.

Green Fact: About a third of the Earth's surface is dry or 'arid', and receives very little rainfall. Dry land becomes dryer when too many animals graze there and people chop down the trees for firewood.

Block of Flats

Build a block of flats full of nosey neighbours who hide behind their curtains as soon as someone sees them peeking out! As well as funny faces, you could draw dogs, cats and other pets at the windows.

RECYCLE:
Cereal box
Thin cardboard

FLATS 1-14.

2 1

1 Cut off the open end of your box. Next, cut a piece of card just a fraction smaller than one of the largest sides of the box.

2 Stand the box up so that the open end becomes the base. Draw several windows, making sure that you leave a space below each window that is the same depth as the window itself.

3 Place the sheet of cardboard inside the box, so that the top of the card sheet meets the top of the box. Hold it against the inside of the windows and draw faces looking out of each. Add open curtains.

4 Pull the cardboard sheet down so that the faces disappear. Hold it against the windows again, and this time paint curtains but no people. Cut off the excess cardboard at the bottom.

5 Take the piece of cardboard out. Paint the block of flats in one colour. When it is dry, paint on some bricks and a door. Add apartment numbers and a street name.

6 Cut a slot in the side of the box at the bottom.

7 Cut a strip of cardboard that sticks out about 5 cm (2 in) from the slot and reaches the middle of the card sheet. Attach it to the back of the card sheet with masking tape, so that when the card handle is resting on the bottom of the slot the windows are empty.

8 To stop the card sheet falling away from the windows, draw and cut out chimney pots with a good-sized tab at their base. Cut a slot along the top front edge of the box for the chimney tab to fit in. Slot your card sheet in front of the tab so that it is held in place.

Clock Tower

This clock tower has a weather vane that spins in the wind. Gently blow on it, or take it outdoors and watch it turn. Make sure that you don't make the clock hands too loose or they will droop.

RECYCLE:

Washing-up liquid bottle
Thick and thin cardboard
Stud paper-fasteners
Used match

Extra items: sandpaper, pump-action hairspray, a mug

1 Prepare the washing-up liquid bottle by rubbing it down with sandpaper then spraying it with hairspray. Paint the conical 'roof' one colour and the rest of the bottle another. When dry, paint or draw on bricks and roof tiles.

2 Draw around a mug on to cardboard. Cut out the circle you have drawn. Make a hole in the centre of the circle. Write in the hours. Start with 12, 3, 6 and 9 at the quarters and then fill in the other numbers.

3 From cardboard, draw and cut out clock hands. Make holes in the circular ends and use a stud paper-fastener to attach them to the centre of the clock face. Glue the clock on to the tower.

4 Cut out and paint cardboard doors that bend open. Draw a door keeper on another piece of card the same size as the doors, and stick this at the base of the tower. Cut out a decorative trim for the roof and paint and attach this too.

5 For the weather vane, draw a cockerel on to card. Cut it out with the small notch in his tummy. Paint it and leave it to dry.

6 Cut out four small squares of cardboard and write on them N for North, E for East, S for South, and W for West. Cut two matching strips of strong cardboard as arms for the weather vane. Cut small notches in the middle of each, and fit them into each other to make a cross. Tape if necessary.

7 Tape the compass points to the end of each arm N, E, S, W as you go around clockwise. Slot the compass cross into the notch at the base of the cockerel.

8 Tape a used match to one side of the cockerel and push the other end into the top of the clock tower so that it can still turn.

Castle and Knights

This wonderful medieval castle is a good project to make over a weekend as it has a papier mâché base, which requires **OVERNIGHT DRYING**. The egg-shell people are quick and easy to make, although you will have to eat lots of eggs to be able to fill the castle!

RECYCLE:
For the Castle
Large, low-sided box
4 washing-up liquid bottles
Thick and thin cardboard
Small cardboard box
Plain white paper
Cocktail sticks
String
Ice-lolly sticks
Newspaper

For the Knights
Toilet-roll tubes
Egg shells
Plastic bottle tops
Thin cardboard

Extra items: flour and water for the **papier mâché** (page 13)

The castle is made from cardboard but the base is built up from papier mâché. Medieval castles were often set on hilltops so that the inhabitants had a clear view of approaching enemies.

1 Make a hinged drawbridge by cutting three slits in the centre of one side of the cardboard box.

2 Cut the tops off the bottles, but make sure they stand taller than the box. Turn them over and mark where to cut slits so that each will fit neatly over a corner. Cut each slit to within 2.5 cm (1 in) of the closed end of the bottle. Fit each bottle over a corner.

3 Cut notches along the top of the box. Cut four strips of cardboard about 5 cm (2 in) deep and long enough to reach around a bottle turret. Cut notches along one long edge of each of these. Tape them to the tops of the turrets.

4 Cut strips of thick cardboard the same length as from one turret to the next and about 6 cm (2 in) deep to form walkways. Make small triangular supports. Space them well apart, and tape them so that they stick out. Rest the walkways on them and tape them to the wall too. Paint them.

5 Take a small box. Cut a strip of cardboard long enough to go around the top of it and about 5 cm (2 in) deep. Cut notches in it and tape in place. Cut out a door to form the keep. Glue it in the centre of the castle base.

6 Make flags for the four turrets out of paper. Cut them to the shape shown above and paint them. When they are dry, attach a cocktail stick with masking tape to the back of each.

7 Make small holes above the drawbridge entrance, and at the top of the drawbridge flap. Attach short lengths of string, as shown, making a small knot behind each hole to keep the string secure.

8 Cut two strips of cardboard, the height of the drawbridge doorway and 2 cm (¾ in) wide and two narrower strips of the same length and glue these behind the wider ones. Glue the thick part of each strip to either side of the doorway, inside the castle. Make a portcullis from ice-lolly sticks that will slip in behind these door posts.

9 Stick the castle on to a large sheet of cardboard. Use papier mâché to build up this base so that you have a moat with banks. Make sure that the drawbridge can reach across the moat.

10 Paint the castle. Paint a piece of newspaper green. When dry, cut strips from it to look like grass and stick them around the base of the castle.

KNIGHTS

1 Cut the toilet-roll tubes crossways into 5 cm (2 in) sections then cut each piece lengthways down one side. Take an egg-shell half for each piece and tape the cardboard tubing around it so that it is held securely.

2 Make lots of egg-shell people and paint some of them to look like knights. You can also make a king and queen with plastic bottle tops as crowns.

Green Fact: Try and ensure that the egg shells you use in these projects are from free-range eggs. Most eggs available in supermarkets are from battery hens, which live in huge sheds in very cramped conditions.

3 Draw a horse on to cardboard. The height at the middle part of the horse's body should be 3 cm (1¼ in). Paint it and cut it out. Make enough horses for riders.

4 Cut 3 cm-long slits at the front and back of each knight. Slot them on to the horses.

Island Town

This fabulous island town takes a little time to make – because the papier mâché has to be left to **DRY OVERNIGHT** – but it is well worth the effort. Once complete, it has roads, train tracks, factories and houses. You can make it a fantasy town, or base it on somewhere you know.

RECYCLE:

2 shallow cardboard boxes, one two-thirds the size of the other
Thick cardboard
Kitchen-roll tube
Newspaper
Small boxes
Cotton wool
Matchbox
Drinking straw

Extra items: flour and water for the **papier mâché** (page 13), twigs, sandpaper

1 Seal both the boxes and tape the smaller box to the middle of the larger one.

Cut a strip of cardboard long enough to run down to the ferry. Paint a road on it and glue it next to the railway tunnel. You can also make your island more realistic by adding sewage pipes, made from pipe cleaners or string, to run down the sides of the island.

2 Stick the boxes in the centre of the flat piece of cardboard. Draw a wiggly line around the edge of it to form the sea. Cut it out.

3 With a black felt-tip pen, draw a railway line around the top edge of the lower box. To make a tunnel over the railway line, cut a triangular section out of the middle of the kitchen-roll tube – be careful not to cut the tube in half. Bend it and tape it as shown. Glue it over the railway line.

4 Make some papier mâché and stick it to the sides of the boxes, taking care to leave the railway line, sea and top of the small box uncovered. Leave the papier mâché somewhere warm to dry before you paint it.

5 While you are waiting for the papier mâché to dry, make some buildings for the town – a factory with cotton wool smoke looks good. Carefully pull the small boxes apart at the seams. Turn them inside out and glue them back into their box shapes so you will have plain cardboard surfaces to paint on.

6 Paint the island and when it is dry glue on a few twigs for trees. Paint the railway line and add roads to the top box. Paint the sea blue and add some beach shapes cut from pieces of very fine sandpaper.

> **Green Fact:** Too much untreated sewage and factory waste continues to be dumped in the sea. When we eat fish that has eaten 'toxic' or poisonous materials, some of those poisons can pass into us.

7 When the paint has dried, glue the buildings on to the island. You can also make a simple ferry from a matchbox, and a station from some card and a drinking straw.

Puppets and Theatres

Here are lots of ideas for making puppets out of all sorts of things: wooden spoons, yoghurt cartons, cardboard, dough, old tights, socks or pieces of wire. Some projects – like the flat puppets – are very simple. Others, such as Ms Smith the glove puppet, need some sewing and you might have to ask a grown-up for help. There are also two theatres to make: a mini one for the finger puppets and a big one for the glove puppets.

RECYCLE:
Large yoghurt carton
Wooden spoon
Plain and patterned fabric
Thick and thin cardboard
Cotton wool
Cocktail stick
Shoe box
String
Cotton thread
Cardboard boxes
Sheet
Buttons
Beads
Toilet-roll tubes
Socks
Plain white paper
Cardboard eggbox
Sweet wrappers
Tights or stockings
Stud paper-fastener
Electrical wire
Clear plastic
Sellotape

Extra items:
a scouring pad
flour and water
a baking tray
a toothbrush
a needle
a mug

SPOON PUPPET

Large yoghurt carton
Wooden spoon
2 small pieces of fabric, of different
    patterns
Thin cardboard
A scouring pad, cotton wool or
    string

Decorate this glamour girl with bits
of jewellery or pieces of foil.

1 Make a hole in the bottom of the yoghurt carton with the points of a pair of scissors. The hole should be big enough for the handle of the spoon to go through easily.

2 Turn the carton the right way up and insert the spoon. Position it so that the 'head' is well above the rim. Cut a strip of fabric that reaches from the top of the carton to the neck of the spoon.

3 Tape the fabric to the outside of the yoghurt carton rim. Join the two ends of fabric with a piece of tape to form a cone.

4 Bunch the fabric around the neck of the spoon and use more tape to secure it.

5 Cut another strip of fabric the same depth as the carton. Position it around the other piece of material and the spoon head. Tape it to the rim of the carton, over the previous piece of tape. Tape the ends to form a cone of material.

107

Green Fact: We know that smoking, and passive smoking, can cause a range of serious illnesses. Another problem is that valuable agricultural land is given over to growing tobacco instead of food crops.

6 Fold down this second layer of material so that the carton and the tape are hidden. Cut out small pieces of fabric and roll them up to make arms. Tape these to the neck of the spoon. Use fabric or coloured paper to make a choker that will cover the tape around the neck.

7 Draw hands and feet on to card and paint them. When dry, cut them out and glue the feet inside the bottom of the skirt and the hands to the ends of the arms. Paint a face on to the spoon. Add a scouring pad, cotton wool, or string for hair.

FINGER PUPPETS

Flour and water for dough
Cocktail stick
Baking tray
Thin cardboard
Toothbrush

These puppets are made from flour and water, and you will need the help of a grown-up to bake them in the oven.

1 Make a dough out of plain flour and water. Add only a little water at a time to make sure the dough does not get too sticky.

2 Put lumps of dough on to a greased baking tray. Mould the dough into faces using the back of a spoon. Use a pencil to make eye holes and a cocktail stick for fine lines. Give the heads long tubular necks.

3 Put the baking tray into an oven at a very low temperature (150 °C/300 °F/Gas 1-2) for half an hour. If after this time the dough has hardened, ask a grown-up to remove it. If not, leave it a little longer and then test again. When the figures are brown and sound hollow when tapped, they are done.

4 When the dough heads are completely cool, paint them. For a cat, make small holes in the face with the cocktail stick and glue in bristles cut from an old toothbrush.

5 Cut strips of cardboard for the characters' bodies. Curl and fix them into tubes that sit comfortably around your fingers. Also cut out and paint pieces such as legs and tails. Glue the neck of each dough head into the top of its cardboard body.

MINI THEATRE

Shoe box
String

Make a mini theatre from a shoe box for the finger puppets to perform in.

1 Stand the shoe box, with its lid on, on end. Paint the whole thing with stripes (including the end the box is standing on). When dry on the outside, paint the inside of the box a different colour. Leave it to dry.

2 With the box still on end and the lid facing away from you, draw a rectangle at the top. It must be large enough for your hand to fit in. Cut along the top and sides of this so that it flaps downwards.

3 Make a hole in the top of the flap and in the front of the box, below where the flap reaches when it is open. Thread string through each hole so that the two pieces can be tied together to keep the flap down.

4 Turn the box around so that the lid side is facing you, and stand it on its other end. Make another flap on this side, also with string ties. This is where the finger puppets will perform.

FLAT PUPPETS

Thin cardboard
Fabric
Cotton thread

Instead of painting the puppets, you can glue on faces cut out of magazines. You could also put together a collage of magazine pieces for the clothing.

1 Invent your own figures, or copy the boy and girl below, on to cardboard. Paint them and when they are dry cut them out, making holes large enough for your fingers.

2 If you like, you can make 'shoes' to cover your fingertips from scraps of fabric tied on with cotton thread.

You can decorate the finger puppets with scraps of fabric. Depending on what you can find, you can create a whole cast of characters. If you have furry fabric you can make a caveman and woman!

HORSE

Toilet-roll tube
Sock
Thin, white cardboard
String
Fabric
Plain white paper

Find a 'horse-coloured' sock for this glove puppet – brown, grey or black look good.

1 Cut a toilet-roll tube in half crossways. In one side of each half cut a hole wide enough for either a couple of fingers or a thumb to fit in. Push both pieces of tube into the end of a sock horizontally, to make a top and bottom lip.

2 Cut a strip of white card and paint lines on it for teeth. Bend the card into a horseshoe shape, and glue it to the sock behind the top lip, so that it fits around your fingers when your hand is inside.

3 Cut two short lengths of string to make curled nostrils. Glue these to the outside of the sock at each end of the upper cardboard-tube lip. Draw, paint and cut out circles for eyes. Glue them in place.

4 Cut out two long ears from cardboard. Cut out pieces of fabric that you can wrap around and glue to them. If you have a matching sock, use that. If you prefer, you can paint them instead.

5 Glue the ears to the back of the horse's head and bend them slightly backwards so that they stand upright.

6 Cut a long strip of paper 5 cm (2 in) wide and paint it the same colour as the horse. When it is dry fold it in half lengthways and cut 2 cm (¾ in) slits all down its length.

7 Cut off the end of the strip and glue it between the ears as a fringe. Glue down the centre of the long strip and attach it along the horse's neck as a mane.

BIRD

Sock
Plain white paper
Buttons or beads
Needle and thread

This big bird with his bright yellow beak is a star performer!

1 Put the sock on your hand, and push it in between your thumb and fingers to make a mouth.

2 Paint a piece of paper yellow. When dry, fold it in half. Cut curves out of the paper where it meets your hand as shown above by the dotted line.

12

3 Fold the front corners of the paper under. Cut off any excess paper and tape it so you have an upper beak.

4 Do the same to make a lower beak, but fold the paper upwards.

5 Sew on buttons or glue on beads for eyes.

6 To make a crest, paint a small piece of paper in a bright colour. When dry, cut it into strips and **curl** them with scissors (page 10). Glue it to the bird's head.

SNAKE

Plain white paper
Sock
Cardboard eggbox

A stripy sock makes a good snake because lots of snakes are stripy in real life.

1 Make a forked tongue out of paper. Put the sock on your hand with the heel part over your thumb and glue the tongue where the mouth will be. When the glue has dried, take off the sock.

2 Make eyes by cutting out two cups from an eggbox and painting them yellow. When they are dry, paint narrow black pupils on them. Put the sock back on your hand and glue the eyes to the side of the snake's head.

DINOSAUR

Thin cardboard
Sock
Sweet wrappers

Instead of using cardboard to make the dinosaur's spines, you can use pieces of felt.

1 Draw eyes on to card and cut them out. Put the sock on your hand with the heel part over your thumb and glue on the eyes. Let the glue dry before taking off the sock.

2 To make spines for the dinosaur, cut a long strip of cardboard and paint it. When it is dry, cut out triangles. Put the glove back on your hand and glue the spines down the dinosaur's back.

3 Cut out and colour a small piece of card for a tongue and some plain white triangles for teeth. Put the sock back on, and glue everything in place.

4 Make spots for your dinosaur by cutting out small circles from sweet wrappers and gluing them all over the head and neck. If you don't have sweet wrappers, paint spots on to card and stick them on instead.

You can make a really cool cat from the foot of a stocking. Use cotton thread to tie the neck, sew the ears and twist a length of nylon into a long tail. Make eyes from card, and whiskers from pipe cleaners.

14

MS SMITH

Tights or stockings
Needle and thread
Thin cardboard
Beads
Plain and patterned fabric
Buttons
Sock
Cotton wool

You may need the help of a grown-up to thread the needle and sew Ms Smith's eyes, mouth, ears and hair. If you have a second old pair of tights you can make her a cat companion.

4 Paint and cut out two cardboard eyes. Glue them in the indents made for eyes. Paint lips where the indent is for the mouth and add eyebrows.

8 For hands and legs, fold or roll up small pieces of nylon. Glue the hands to the ends of the sleeves, and the legs to the inside front of the dress. Cut out and paint cardboard shoes. When dry, glue them to the end of the legs.

1 Loosely roll up the leg of an old pair of tights. Cut off the other leg half way down. Continue to fold the leg up until it is in a ball that can be stuffed into the half-leg. This will make the head.

2 Tie cotton thread around a portion of the stuffed stocking to make a nose.

3 With your finger, push a hole in the stocking for an eye, and then sew thread over it, to make an indent. Do the same for the other eye and for a mouth.

5 Pull pieces of nylon outwards to form ears and stitch them to hold them in place. Glue on beads for earrings.

6 Cut a piece of fabric about 18 x 23 cm (7 x 9 in). Lay it down with the wrong side facing you. Fold it in half and put glue down one of the longest edges. Also put glue in a sloping line at the top where the neck and shoulders will be.

7 When the glue is dry, turn the rectangle of fabric inside out so that the right side of the material is showing. Roll some scraps of material into tubes and glue them to the dress as sleeves.

115

9 Slide the dress over your hand and push one or two fingers into the head – this is how you will hold the puppet. Carefully glue the neck inside the dress. Make a collar and cuffs for the dress from scraps of plain fabric or card and glue them on. You can also sew buttons down the middle.

10 To make hair, cut the end off a sock and pad it with more scraps of fabric or cotton wool. Thread a needle. Make an initial stitch then twist the cotton around this top knot and secure it with a few stitches. Shape the remainder of the sock around the head and glue or sew it in place.

Green Fact: Before getting a cat, a dog or any other pet, think about the consequences. Animals need attention every day of their lives and they live a very long time. Remember, animals are not toys.

THEATRE

Large, rectangular cardboard box
Thin cardboard
Sheet
Plain and patterned fabric

Put on a play for your friends in this traditional theatre. It even has an authentic proscenium arch – the decorative arch that separates the audience from the stage.

1 Lay the box, largest side down, in the middle of a big piece of cardboard and draw around it. Remove the box.

2 Using this shape as a guide (shown here by the dotted line) draw the arch. Make the plain inner frame about 5 cm (2 in) smaller than the rectangle you have drawn, and the fancy outer arch about 3 cm (1¼ in) bigger. Cut it out.

3 Stand the box on its narrow edge with the large closed side facing you. Position the arch in front of it and draw around the inner frame on to the box. Cut out the middle of the box.

4 Paint the arch yellow and leave it to dry.

5 Glue the arch on to the front of the theatre. When the glue has dried, paint the bottom border of the box so it matches the arch.

6 Cut the sheet so that it is as wide as the bottom of the box, and hangs down far enough to hide the puppeteer. Paint it with stripes and, when dry, glue it to the bottom of the box. Cut two pieces of fabric and stick the top edges inside the front of the box. Cut two more strips of material and glue them around the middle of each curtain.

7 Cut another piece of material (a plain, dark colour is best) the same width as the box, but a little longer. This is a flap to hide the puppeteer. Tape or glue it to the back of the box at the top.

8 Stand the theatre on a chair or low stool and you are ready to perform.

To produce the best effect, suspend a white sheet in front of a light. Move the shadow puppets between the light and the sheet and your audience will see them moving in mid-air like magic.

BIRD

Thin cardboard
Stud paper-fastener
Electrical wire or newspaper

Move the wire or newspaper rods, and make the bird fly.

1 Draw the outline of a bird with a feathery tail and one wing on to a piece of card. Cut them out and cut out an eye.

2 Draw around the wing shape on to another piece of card and cut it out to make a second wing. Make small holes in each of the wings and one in the bird's body. Attach the wings to the body with a stud paper-fastener. One wing should face forwards and the other backwards.

3 Tape pieces of wire to the ends of the wings and the bottom of the body. (If you don't have any wire, tightly roll up sheets of newspaper and tape them together to make rods.) Move them and make the bird fly.

CYCLIST

Thick and thin cardboard
A mug

Follow steps 1 and 2 to make a man on a bike. Steps 3 and 4 show you how to make a second pair of wheels. If you hold the cyclist with one hand and move the wheels behind him with the other, the wheels seem to turn.

1 Draw the outline of a man on a bicycle on to thin card. Trace round a mug to draw even-sized wheels.

18

FACE

Electrical wire
Clear plastic
Sellotape

Electrical wire is easy to bend into all kinds of interesting shapes and is perfect for making funny faces.

Instead of using clear plastic and sellotape for the face, you can use clingfilm.

1 Begin the face by making a big circle of wire. Bend and twist more wire to make ears, eyes a nose and mouth and curly hair.

2 Stick clear plastic over the hair, mouth and eyes with sellotape and use felt-tipped pens to colour it.

2 Cut out the figure and the spaces between the spokes of the wheels.

3 Using the same mug as in step 1, draw and cut out a second set of wheels.

4 Make a stick out of thick card, bend the end and tape it to the cyclist. Make a second holder and tape it to the extra wheels.

Orchestra

Forget the piano lessons! You can create a whole orchestra out of rubbish that is just lying around waiting to be used. Empty detergent bottles filled with dried beans make instant maracas and a piece of hose piping makes a great tuba. But remember, these instruments can be as loud as the real thing and not everyone will appreciate the music so always ask for permission before performing.

RECYCLE:

Plastic bottles
Toilet-roll tubes
Plain white paper
Thick cardboard
Elastic bands
Aluminium foil
String
Fabric
Foil tops

Cotton thread
Kitchen-roll tube
Tissue paper
Coloured paper

Extra items: dried beans, peas or rice, a baking tray, a needle, a length of garden hose, a plastic funnel, biscuit tins

MARACAS

Plastic bottles
Dried beans, peas or rice
Toilet-roll tubes
Plain white paper

Don't put too many beans in the bottle or they won't make such a good clatter. About a handful should do.

20

You can make a xylophone from bottles filled with different amounts of water. Put food colouring in the water to make it more attractive. Play the bottles with two pencils. The fullest bottles will have the lowest note, and the emptiest the highest note. Blowing into the water with a straw makes a bubbly noise.

1 Clean out the bottles and leave them to dry thoroughly. If you have one, use a funnel to get the beans into the bottle without spilling them. Tape the top back on.

2 Tape a toilet-roll tube over the bottle top. This will be the handle of your maraca, so it must be securely fastened.

3 Wrap some paper around the bottle and fasten it over the base of the toilet-roll tube. Tape it down the side and paint it. Paint the handle the same colour.

SCREECHER
Plain white paper

An ordinary piece of paper is all that you need to make a great screeching sound. Don't blow it too close to anyone's ear!

1 Cut an oblong of paper and fold it in half, then in half again. Tear a very small hole in the middle. Hold the paper against your face making sure that the middle pieces of paper are touching each other, and blow hard.

GUITAR

Thick cardboard
Elastic bands
Baking tray
Aluminium foil
String
Fabric

This guitar has a sound box and strings to pluck. You might have to ask a grown-up to make sure the strap is the right length for you.

1 Find a large sheet of cardboard, or open out a cardboard box, and draw the outline of a guitar.

2 Carefully cut it out, making a hole in the middle.

3 Choose a deep baking tray that is a little wider than the hole in the guitar. Wrap the elastic bands lengthwise around the tray then tape it to the back of the guitar.

4 Paint the guitar and when it is dry decorate it with silver stars cut out of aluminium foil. Glue string along the neck of the guitar as far as the hole.

5 Decide whether you are a left-handed or right-handed guitarist then make two small holes in the guitar with scissors. Thread a strip of fabric around your shoulders and knot it through the holes to make a shoulder strap.

BUZZER

Plain white paper

Instead of plain paper you can use a sheet of newspaper, but make sure it is clean. The flap of paper will vibrate and make a funny buzzing noise through the tube.

1 Roll up a sheet of thin paper to make a long, thin tube. Tape it securely then paint it.

2 Make a cut at one end of the tube. Make a second, diagonal cut from the first cut to the end of the tube. Now the end will be pointed. Fold down the pointed end. Trim the other end to make it neat, put it to your lips and suck.

SHAKER

Foil tops
Cotton thread
Kitchen-roll tube

You'll need lots of foil tops from milk bottles or plastic bottles for this project. Ask a grown-up for help threading the needle.

1 Thread the needle and tie a big knot at the end of the cotton. Carefully put the foil lids on the point of the needle and push them along the thread. Do a few threads and tape the knotted ends securely.

2 Decorate a long cardboard tube and leave it to dry.

(Continued overleaf)

WHISTLE

Kitchen-roll tube
Tissue paper
Elastic band

If you have a few kitchen-roll tubes you can make several whistles. Cut them down to different lengths and they'll make different sounds.

3 Tape the loose ends of cotton to the top of the tube and your shaker is ready.

1 Make evenly spaced holes along a kitchen-roll tube with a pair of scissors.

Encourage your friends to make instruments too and then you can have a complete band.

Green Fact: We don't often think of noise as being a form of pollution, but it is. Noise is measured in decibels so a whisper is 20 decibels, a conversation is 50 decibels and a jet aircraft is 110 decibels.

2 Paint the tube, but don't block the holes.

3 When it has dried, hold a piece of tissue paper tightly over one end of the tube and fasten it in place with an elastic band. Blow down the other end and the tissue will vibrate and make a noise.

TUBA

Length of garden hose
Plastic funnel
Coloured paper

You should ask a grown-up to cut a length of garden hose for you. Make sure it is a piece that has never been used to spread weed-killer or any other pesticides. These could make you very ill.

1 Push a plastic funnel into one end of a short length of garden hose. If you don't have a funnel, cut the top off a plastic bottle and use this. Tape it to the hose.

2 Cut strips of coloured paper and wind them around the hose. Cut dots and glue these on to the funnel. Blow, talk, sing and hum into the pipe moving the funnel around your head to vary the sound.

DRUMS

Biscuit tins
Coloured paper
Aluminium foil
Fabric

Wooden spoons make excellent drum sticks. These drums make a lot of noise, so make sure you only play them when you won't disturb anyone.

1 Decorate the biscuit tins by wrappping them in coloured paper, or plain paper that you then paint. Tape a smaller tin to the side of a big one.

2 Paint over the tape and cut out silver stars from foil and stick these around the tins. If you want to walk with the drums, cut a strip of fabric long enough to go round your neck and tape it to the edges of the larger drum.

This amazing balloon is made from papier mâché, which you must leave to DRY OVERNIGHT. Sit the egg-shell pilot inside the basket and suspend the balloon on a piece of string from the ceiling.

RECYCLE:
Plastic bottle
Plain white paper
String
2 toilet-roll tubes
Egg shell
Fabric
Buttons

Extra items: a balloon, flour and water for the **papier mâché** (page 13)

1 Blow up a balloon – you might need the help of a grown-up to inflate it completely.

2 Cover the balloon in two or three layers of papier mâché.

3 Set the balloon aside and leave it to dry overnight.

4 Paint the papier mâché. When it is dry, poke something sharp into the end of the balloon to pop it and pull out any bits of rubber you can see.

5 To make a basket for the pilot, cut the base off a plastic bottle. Cut a strip of paper as deep as the base and draw a basket pattern on it. Tape it around the base.

6 Cut four lengths of string. Make small holes in the basket and knot the string through them. Glue the other ends to the balloon. Glue a piece of string to the top of the balloon to hang it up with.

7 Now make a pilot. Cut a third off two toilet-roll tubes then cut these down the middle. Open up the halves and wrap them tightly around half an egg shell. Tape them in position.

8 Give the pilot goggles, a helmet and a smiling face. Leave the egg shell to dry.

9 Cut a strip of fabric wide enough to wrap around the pilot and tape it in place. Make rolls of fabric for arms and glue them to the body. Cut out paper hands and glue these to the arms. Add buttons to the suit.

Mobiles

Mobiles are quick and easy to make and will liven up any room, although you will need the help of a grown-up to hang them. You can make stars and a rocket – complete with astronaut – or a collection of birds and insects. Look at the mobiles on these pages and see what ideas you come up with.

RECYCLE:
For the Bird
Thin cardboard
Plain white paper
String

For the Rocket
Thin cardboard
Toilet-roll tube
String

For the Star
Thin cardboard
String

For the Spider
Cardboard eggbox
Plain white paper
Thin cardboard

For the Bee
Toilet-roll tubes
Plain white paper
Tights or stockings
Electrical wire

Extra items: coat hangers, a mug

BIRD

1 On a piece of card, draw the outline of a bird. Paint it and when it is dry cut it out.

2 To make wings, paint a piece of paper that is as long as the bird. When it is dry, turn it over and paint the other side.

3 Fold the paper lengthwise like a fan.

4 Cut a narrow, vertical slot as wide as the wings in the side of the bird.

5 Thread the paper wings through the slot and open them out. Make a small hole and thread a piece of string through it.

6 Make several birds and tie them on to two coat hangers or two sticks taped into a cross. Put some of the birds on long strings and others on shorter ones to make the mobile more interesting.

ROCKET

1 Make fins for the rocket out of thin card. Cut slots in them and slide them about a third of the way up a toilet-roll tube. Paint everything white.

2 Decorate the rocket and draw the face of an astronaut looking out of a window.

3 Now make the rocket's nose cone. Make a circle by tracing around a mug on to card. Cut it out, cut a slot up to the middle and bend it into a cone. Tape it, glue it to the rocket and paint it. To hang it up, make a hole near the top, thread a piece of string through and knot it on the inside.

STAR

1 Trace around a mug on to thin cardboard then cut out the disc you have drawn. To measure the circumference of the disc, wrap a piece of string around the mug then hold it against a ruler. Divide this by five and mark this measurement on the disc.

2 Draw lines from the five points to make an even star. Cut this out and use it as a template for other stars. Now cut up the point of one star and up the middle of another. Slot them together. Tape a piece of string to the top to hang them up.

SPIDER

1 Cut off one of the cups from a cardboard eggbox and paint it black. Leave it to dry. Draw eyes and a mouth on paper, cut them out and stick them on to the spider.

2 Make eight legs out of thin card and paint them black. When they are dry, make tiny slits in the body of the spider, slot the legs through and tape them on the inside.

BEE

1 Paint a toilet-roll tube in stripes of yellow and black. While you are waiting for it to dry, cut out eyes and a mouth from paper. Glue them on.

2 To make wings for the bee, cut two pieces of nylon from a pair of tights. Wrap them round strips of wire bent into wing shapes and glue them to the back of the bee.

Fish Tank

With a big jam jar and some card, you can have a brilliant collection of exotic sea creatures. Once you have made the tropical fish and an octopus, why not try making a sea horse, a whale or a mermaid?

RECYCLE:

A large glass jar
Thick and thin cardboard
Cotton thread
Cotton wool

Extra item: food colouring

32

1 Put the neck of the jar on to a piece of card and trace around it. Cut out a circle slightly bigger than the one you have drawn. Next, put some food colouring into the jar and roll it around so that the inside is coated. Leave it to dry.

2 Draw some fish and funny sea creatures. Colour them in then cut them out. If you like, paint the other side.

3 Glue cotton thread to one side of the sea creatures. Make tiny holes in the cardboard lid, thread the pieces of cotton through and tape them down. Paint the lid.

4 To make seaweed, draw wiggly lines on to the paper. Paint them and when they are dry cut them out.

5 If the jar is very wide and you are using two sheets of paper, tape them together. Curl them up and drop them into the jar.

6 Cut out a boat from thin card. Give it a card support that will bend back and hold the boat upright. Glue some cotton wool smoke to the funnels then tape the boat to the lid. Carefully put the lid on the jar.

Fish Kite

Run with the fish kite behind you and see it fill with air and fly! You can play with it indoors, but outdoors on a breezy day is best. Ask a grown-up to cut and bend the wire for you.

RECYCLE:

A square of white sheeting,
   approx. 50 x 50 cm
    (20 x 20 in)
Wire
Tissue paper
   or thin fabric
String

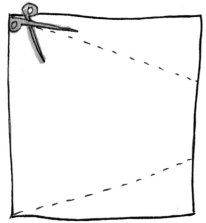

1 Cut the sheet so that one end is slightly narrower than the other.

2 Paint the fish. Give it scales, fins, eyes and a mouth. Leave it to dry.

3 Ask a grown-up to cut you two pieces of wire just larger than the two ends and tape them into hoops.

Special Pensioners' Hearing Aid!

A new hearing aid has been introduced for Pensioners. The invention is low cost, simple to operate and brings IMPROVED hearing to virtually everyone!

THE EFFECT IS IMMEDIATE. NO FUSS, NO BOTHER

The sound is crisp and clear and you will be astonished just how easily conversations, television or radio can be heard with such a small device!

SPECIAL BENEFITS FOR EXISTING HEARING AID USERS!

If you already wear a hearing aid, either 'over the ear' or 'right inside the ear', then you will be interested in this economical device.

DON'T WAIT ANOTHER MINUTE

To learn for yourself about this remarkable device for clearer hearing! Simply complete the coupon overleaf for further helpful information and free illustrated booklet specially written for the Hard of Hearing.

REMEMBER...

This information pack is free, without any obligation and will be sent by return of post! Simply telephone or send the FREEPOST application overleaf.

No Stamp Required

Hidden Hearing
FREEPOST MA117/003
Medway Street
MAIDSTONE
Kent
ME14 1BR

4 Using double-sided tape, tape the sheet into a long tube. Next, tape the hoops inside the ends of the fish by folding and taping the material over the wire.

5 Make streamers out of strips of coloured tissue paper or thin fabric and glue them along the spine and around the tail.

6 Make a little hole either side of the fish's mouth and tie on two pieces of string. Tie these to a longer piece of string and you are ready to go!

Credits

With thanks to Ayesha Bulbulia,
Lauren Fried, Daniel George
and Shola Morphet for their help
demonstrating the projects in this book.

040-634-2